PRESIDING IDEAS IN WORDSWORTH'S POETRY

by

MELVIN M. RADER

*"The mind, mingling with the noblest of the senses,
and becoming one with them, may be truly called the
salvation of all."*—Plato, *Laws,* Jowett's translation.

GORDIAN PRESS
NEW YORK
1968

PR 5888
R3
1968

Originally Published 1931
Reprinted 1968

Library Of Congress Catalog Card Number: 68-8341
Published By Gordian Press

To

FREDERICK MORGAN PADELFORD

ACKNOWLEDGMENT

I take pleasure in thanking *Modern Philology* for permission to reproduce portions of my article, *The Transcendentalism of William Wordsworth,* which appeared in November, 1928. To Katherine Rader I am much indebted for criticism and final preparation of the manuscript. My gratitude for valuable suggestions is extended to Professors Finley M. Foster and Lyon N. Richardson of Western Reserve University, and to Professors William Savery, Allen R. Benham, and Frederick M. Padelford of the University of Washington. I am especially grateful to Dr. Padelford for a seminar in Wordsworth which supplied the orientation needed for my project.

In the field of books, my chief obligation is to Ernest de Selincourt's variorum edition of *The Prelude*. The publication therein of the early manuscript versions of the poem has disclosed a large body of material never before available to the public. This fresh evidence permits a determination of the poet's views with an exactitude and completeness quite impossible hitherto.

MELVIN M. RADER

Seattle, Washington

CONTENTS

I

THE INFLUENCE OF COLERIDGE

The death of Coleridge was announced to us by his friend Wordsworth. It was the Sunday evening after the death occurred that my brother and I walked over to the Mount, where we found the Poet alone. One of the first things we heard from him was the death of one who had been, he said, his friend for more than thirty years. He then continued to speak of him; called him the most *wonderful* man he had ever known—wonderful for the originality of his mind, and the power he possessed of throwing off in profusion grand central truths from which might be evolved the most comprehensive systems. . . .Though a considerable period had elapsed during which they had not seen much of each other, Coleridge and he had been, uninterruptedly, in as close intimacy as man could be with man.

Reverend R. P. Graves[1]

I

We can scarcely speak of Wordsworth's "philosophy" unless we stretch the meaning of the word. Certainly he was not so philosophical as Lucretius, who celebrated the teachings of Epicurus; or as Dante, who transfigured the system of St. Thomas Aquinas; or as Goethe, who glorified the pantheism of Spinoza. Yet he had the ability to organize all his experience in the light of ever-presiding ideas; he had the faculty of co-ordinating everything he knew in an expression of life's total meaning. This thoughtfulness in his writing was in consonance with his genius, for his was a wonderfully philosophical imagination and a very rare capacity to blend the incidents of living into a major organism of meaning and relation. He intentionally fused meditation into his poetry, believing that the interpretation of reality fell within the province of the poet.[2] In a quite untechnical sense, therefore, we can say that Wordsworth had a philosophy.

Until recently the philosophy of the earlier Wordsworth was misrepresented by a late version of *The Prelude*. But we now have the early manuscripts which place their author in a true light. He consequently seems a bolder and a less ambiguous thinker. His mystical excitement is more evident. His early animism and pantheism are revealed far more completely. We more clearly grasp his ruling idea: his sense of the coherence of all being, oneness in interdependence and oneness in spiritual substance. In the course of this chapter, moreover, we shall discover that the new manuscripts render unmistakable the great influence of Coleridge.

1

This disclosure is exactly what we might expect. For in view of Coleridge's endowments and the circumstances of his intimacy, he must surely have moulded his friend's mind more fully than any other thinker. His memory and erudition and his brilliance in discussion amazed his contemporaries and deepened his influence. Insatiable thirst for philosophic studies equipped him with the grand central truths which he bestowed upon his acquaintances.

Wordsworth's susceptibility to the Coleridgean influence was heightened by the love that bound together the two friends:

> There is no grief, no sorrow, no despair,
> No languor, no dejection, no dismay,
> No absence scarcely can there be, for those
> Who love as we do.[3]

Not only profound affection, but the breakdown of convictions, rendered Wordsworth's mind highly impressionable. When he fell under the sway of his friend's intellect, he was just emerging from a stage of extreme intellectual disorganization. This was his "soul's last and lowest ebb," when his faith in Godwinism had crumbled and he had given "up moral questions in despair." The crisis occurred in 1795, but the poet's bewilderment gave way slowly. It was precisely at this most strategic of all times that Coleridge extended aid. At the very period when Wordsworth was yearning for light, a friend appeared with a wealth of philosophical knowledge and an eager proselytizing spirit.[4] During 1797-1798, the two poets were in "as close intimacy as man could be with man." These years of deepest friendship were probably the most formative in the career of both writers. So completely did they share their ideas that they seemed to Wordsworth as "Twins almost in genius and in mind!"[5] Under the stimulus of this solidarity, each leaned heavily upon his companion for guidance in composition.[6] In their endless hours of talk, the expansive mind of Coleridge must have invigorated his comrade's entire mental life.

II

Fortunately the evidence is sufficiently precise to furnish definite insight into the nature of this influence. We have direct testimony, for example, that Wordsworth abandoned necessitarianism as a result of Coleridge's persuasion.

The doctrine of necessity, which denies free will to man, had been adopted by both poets during their devotion to William God-win. But at an early period Coleridge manifested a repugnance to the conception. This aversion is indicated by his plan for a series of "Hymns" which he had in preparation during 1796-1797. In the first record of his intention, apparently written as early as June, 1796, he decried "the Godwinian System of Pride," which made man "an outcast of blind Nature ruled by a fatal Necessity."[7] This distaste for necessitarianism matured, and in March, 1801, was announced in a letter to a friend, Thomas Poole.[8]

After a time, his attitude affected Wordsworth. In another letter written to Poole, January 15, 1804, he said:

> I love and honour you, Poole, for many things—scarcely for anything more than that, trusting in the rectitude and simplicity of your own heart . . . .you never suffered either my subtlety, or my eloquence, to proselytize you to the pernicious doctrine of Necessity. All praise to the Great Being who has graciously enabled me to find my way out of that labyrinth-den of sophistry, and, I would fain believe, to bring with me a better clue than has hitherto been known, to enable others to do the same. I have convinced Southey and Wordsworth, and W., as you know, was even to extravagance, a Necessitarian.[9]

Thus Coleridge persuaded his friend into a reversal of opinion upon one of the most fundamental of all human problems. The idea of freedom was made basic in Wordsworth's subsequent poetry. All of nature—the "human Mind," the "little Meadow flower," the grand "Forest tree," the "Soul of all the worlds"—was thought to be free, active, alive, palpitating with "its own divine vitality."[10]

III

Coleridge's rejection of necessitarianism was incidental to his escape from the system of eighteenth century psychology. In the associationists, such as William Godwin and David Hartley, he had found an easy explanation of mental states. The "associational psychology" rested upon the theory that it is possible to find the beginning of a thing in terms of its constituents; or to use other words, that the origin may be discovered in the composition of the parts. According to this view, a thought or emotion is simply the summation of very small units— ideas or sensations.

The conception may be clarified by contrast with the opposing theory. It is given to the musician, said Browning, "that out of three sounds he frame, not a fourth sound, but a star." There is no mere addition of sounds; there is a sheer creation. Within the mind the process is more complex. Mental growth is determined not only by creative synthesis, but by the functioning of an active mind, a self-consciousness, that exists prior to sensation. Thought does not originate in sense; it arises within the mind under stimulus. Consciousness receives the sense impressions and utilizes them in its own generative, form-building activities.

Therefore the resultant mental processes are not to be exhaustively analysed into their constituents for two reasons: First, the synthesis is more than the parts, a chord is more than the individual sounds, a boy's love is more than the kiss, the sweet words, and the warm silences. Second, the thoughts and feelings are possessed by a mind, fused into the tissue of self-consciousness; the love is not any love, it is *the boy's* love, part and parcel of his being, expressive of his essence. To find its origin, in the radical sense, would be to discover the beginning of his mind. These two difficulties in the way of analytical psychology are overlooked by associationism, which supposes that there is nothing before the mind which does not derive from sensation.

Coleridge was not the man to cling to any such psychology. From the time of his boyhood he was averse to seeing the mind and nature as "a mass of little things."[11] Except during a temporary aberration when he was enamoured of Hartley, he had all the romanticist's hatred of rationalistic psychology, with its extreme dependence upon analysis.[12] As early as 1796 he was convinced that the problem of origin is too complex to solve by a mere resolution of a whole into its parts.[13] Disentanglement from the entire theory followed. He announced in a letter of March 16, 1801, that he had overthrown the doctrine of associationism.[14] A letter written to Southey more than two years later is equally emphatic. The same message sets forth a theory of memory wholly un-Hartleian.[15] Fourteen years after, in the *Biographia Literaria* of 1817, Coleridge was still denouncing associationism.[16]

Though the evidence is slight, Wordsworth must have learned a good deal from Coleridge about the associational psychology, at first in praise, but soon in depreciation. The two friends united in their mature convictions, not entirely rejecting associationism, but modifying and subordinating it. This agreement is indicated by the following address of Wordsworth to Coleridge:

Who knows the individual hour in which
His habits were first sown, even as a seed?
Who that shall point as with a wand and say
This portion of the river of my mind
Came from yon fountain?' Thou, my Friend! art one
More deeply read in thy own thoughts; to thee
Science appears but what in truth she is,
Not as our glory and our absolute boast,
But as a succedaneum, and a prop
To our infirmity. No officious slave
Art thou of that false secondary power
By which we multiply distinctions, then
Deem that our puny boundaries are things
That we perceive, and not that we have made.
To thee, unblinded by these formal arts,
The unity of all hath been revealed,
And thou wilt doubt, with me less aptly skilled
Than many are to range the faculties
In scale and order, class the cabinet
Of their sensations, and in voluble phrase
Run through the history and birth of each
As of a single independent thing.
Hard task, vain hope, to analyse the mind,
If each most obvious and particular thought,
Not in a mystical and idle sense,
But in the words of Reason deeply weighed,
Hath no beginning.[17]

Wordsworth shared Coleridge's belief that it is vain to search for the beginning of a thing, especially of a thought, and that the analysis of complexes into their components, which are regarded as ultimate and exhaustive of the whole, is a blind and servile procedure; because often the parts are merged and lost in the creative synthesis of the whole.

Especially significant in the quotation is Wordsworth's emphasis upon the unity of consciousness. Thought has no beginning, because it is rooted in the mind, an integer to itself, which is implicated in each mental process. To find the beginning, therefore, would be to find the origin of the mind itself,—to trace back an infinite regress since mental characteristics are hereditary. In this very fundamental conception the two poets agree; Coleridge must either have confirmed his friend's independent point of view or else must have converted him. In any event, we have this tribute to Coleridge's wisdom, which clearly impressed Wordsworth.

IV

The distaste for associationism was connected with a liking for what is virtually its contrary, transcendentalism.[18] Coleridge's predilection for a transcendental philosophy is forecast in his poem of 1796, *The Destiny of Nations,* in which he writes of the "indwelling angel guide" that directed Joan of Arc and of the uncertain, symbolical value of sense experience. In *Religious Musings,* another poem of the same period, the author himself is represented as perceiving the present deity, not by a discursive process, but by a mystic's immediate apprehension. Also an early Memorandum Book, written by Coleridge between the spring of 1795 and the spring or summer of 1798, contains several notations of a transcendentalist drift.[19] His point of view, as time went on, was broadened and systematized. In March 1801 he wrote that "all truth is a species of revelation," a statement which suggests how wide a compass he allotted to the transcendental mind. After his study of Kant, his ideas became more precise:

We learn all things indeed by *occasion* of experience; but the very facts so learnt force us inward on the antecedents, that must be pre-supposed in order to render experience itself possible.[20]

His basic notion was that man is equipped with a transcendental faculty of "pure Reason, which dictates unconditionally,"[21] and which "affirms truths which no sense could perceive, nor experiment verify, nor experience confirm."[22] In *The Friend,* partially written in Wordsworth's own home, he objects to an empirical, hedonistic morality, because it is not based upon that "part of our nature which in all men may and ought to be the same,—in the conscience and the common sense."[23]

Wordsworth also announces that men have "One Sense for moral judgments, as one eye, For the sun's light."[24] In *The Convention of Cintra,* composed in 1808, he speaks of the "dictates of paramount and infallible conscience." Surely infallible dictates do not derive solely from the incomplete and fallible evidence of experience. In the last lines of *The Prelude,* Wordsworth again implies the operation of transcendental factors:

> what we have loved
> Others will love, and we will teach them how;
> Instruct them how the mind of man becomes
> A thousand times more beautiful than the earth
> On which he dwells, above this frame of things
> . . . .
> In beauty exalted, as it is itself
> Of quality and fabric more divine.

Thus Wordsworth proposes to join hands with Coleridge in promoting the point of view which both of them maintain. It would seem that the outlook thus expressed rests upon a transcendental foundation. If the mind is a thousand times more beautiful than the earth, if the spiritual faculties are immeasurably more divine than the external world, presumably there must be some internal, supersensuous factors in knowledge. But fortunately we are not left to even this fairly safe conjecture. Wordsworth definitely announced that he is indebted to Coleridge for his conception of "duty" and "a Reason which indeed is reason."[25]

V

The passage in which the reference to duty and reason is made needs to be very carefully scrutinized, for it refers also to Wordsworth's change of opinion in regard to pantheism. This alteration was subsequent to a similar reversal in Coleridge's beliefs. It is well known that the latter passed through a stage of pantheism from which he gradually emerged. When he finally abandoned his pantheistic faith, he immediately tried to convert Wordsworth, then a pantheist, but at first with no great success.[26] In course of time, however, he did bring about a change in conviction. Although Wordsworth, like Coleridge himself, still believed in a "mighty unity," he modified his earlier ideas at his friend's instigation:

> With such a theme,
> Coleridge! with this my argument, of thee
> Shall I be silent? O most loving Soul!
> Placed on this earth to love and understand,
> And from thy presence shed the light of love,
> Shall I be mute ere thou be spoken of?
> Thy gentle Spirit to my heart of hearts
> Did also find its way; and thus the life
> Of all things and the mighty unity
> In all which we behold, and feel, and are,

> Admitted more habitually a mild
> Interposition, and closelier gathering thoughts
> Of man and his concerns, such as become
> A human Creature, be he who he may!
> Poet, or destined for a humbler name;
> And so the deep enthusiastic joy,
> The rapture of the Hallelujah sent
> From all that breathes and is, was chasten'd, stemm'd
> And balanced by a Reason which indeed
> Is reason; duty and pathetic truth;
> And God and Man divided, as they ought,
> Between them the great system of the world
> Where Man is sphered, and which God animates.[27]

This is one of the most important passages among those confined to the 1805-1806 *Prelude*. It makes abundantly clear that Wordsworth passed through two stages, pantheistic and theistic, although he maintained a bias from first to last against an absentee God.

The recognition that Wordsworth did change his mind is prerequisite to the interpretation of his thought. An attempt to force all of his poetry into a consistent whole is simply an effort at mutilation. The valid approach, which recognizes the rich variety of his thought and the kinetic nature of his development, discloses a man in place of an effigy. Once we have recognized the diversity of Wordsworth's poetry, we can more readily correlate his growth with the shifting philosophy of his friend.

A great deal might be written concerning the other opinions of Coleridge: his insistence upon the active character of the mind;[28] his recognition of the deep subliminal self which vitalizes consciousness;[29] his tendency toward an emotionalistic interpretation of man and nature;[30] his conception of the mighty unity of all being;[31] and his mature view that reality as a whole is spiritual in substance. These opinions are all approximated or exhibited in Wordsworth's poetry.

VI

The beliefs of Coleridge presented in this chapter were formulated before 1806. Of the quotations cited, indeed, a considerable proportion bear upon the period 1796-1799, when the seminal principles of Wordsworth's art and thought were being formulated. Other influences came later, but all were sufficiently early to affect some of Wordsworth's greatest poetry.   We have seen that Coleridge overthrew necessitarianism, revised associationism, adopted a transcendental solution of the problem of knowledge, and changed from pantheism to an immanent theism.   And Wordsworth attained, with Coleridge's assistance, to substantially the same philosophy. Explicit statements to that effect, exact similarities between their views, leave scarcely any room for doubt.   Let us recall Wordsworth's own statement quoted at the beginning of the chapter: the two brother poets were "Twins almost in genius and in mind!" Wordsworth may have overestimated that similarity, for he had a tougher, more conservative and realistic mind than Coleridge.   Yet their community of heart and intellect remains one of the undying wonders of literary history.

II

THE DEVELOPMENT OF WORDSWORTH'S PERSONALITY

The higher mode of being does not exclude, but necessarily includes, the lower; the intellectual does not exclude, but necessarily includes, the sentient; the sentient, the animal; and the animal, the vital—to its lowest degrees.

WORDSWORTH[1]

In the previous chapter we have looked for the source of Wordsworth's thought in the influence of Coleridge. We have now to investigate a still more important source, the poet's own personality. Our inquiry will be most fruitful if we study his mind in its unfoldment; we can thus more readily discern the strength and constancy of the forces which operated upon him.

What is most impressive about his development is not its differentiation into chronological divisions, but its inner cohesion and continuity. We shall nevertheless find it convenient, for the sake of a fuller analysis, to accept a provisional schematization based upon *The Prelude*:

Childhood Age 1-10	1. *Stage of Sensation.* This is the period of glad animal movements. The reflective faculties are undeveloped. The visionary gleam rests on the child's perceptions, and an incipient mysticism appears.	Child's own body and mind
Boyhood Age 10-17	2. *Stage of Emotion.* At first there is an unconscious drinking in of beauty, of which the mind gradually becomes conscious. Fear and awe are uppermost. The creative and mystical tendencies persist.	Nature
Youth Age 17-22	3. *Stage of Fancy.* Mind, attempting to to be creative, indulges in conceits and forced associations. All nature is given a moral life.	Nature
Early Manhood Age 22-26	4. *Stage of Reason as a Faculty of Judgment.* This is the period of republican ardour. In the later stages, Godwin is accepted, and a crisis follows. Nature is approached analytically. The senses become despotic.	Man

11

Maturity Age 26-34	5. *Stage of Imagination and the Grand and Simple Reason.* Man is still primary, but the old love of nature is renewed and deepened. Fear no longer dominates; calm and meditation are in control. There is a new sense of the oneness of man and nature, a oneness in God; and also a new sense of the value of the homely and familiar.	Man+ Nature—

It is to be understood, of course, that each stage has not an exclusive set of characteristics. There may be anticipation in one period of traits that become pronounced only at a later time. Also the values developed in the successive periods tend to persist, so that in the last stage there is completeness, synchronization, and mutual protection among the mental powers.

I. Childhood: The Stage of Sensation

At the earliest time of life the germs are present which will develop into the highest faculties of being. From the very first creative sensibilities are at work; there is an initial activity—a "poetic spirit" which works in alliance with the stimulation from the encircling world. The infant is eager, prompt, and watchful, or the stuff of his experience will be loath to coalesce. Being endowed with this original fund of sensitivity, he proceeds to gather passion from his mother's eye, and pleasure in her arms and at her breast; these feelings send an awakening breeze through his perceptions; they irradiate and exalt the objects of sensation. Thus the tiny mind, "even as an agent of one great mind," creates as well as receives; for it is "an inmate of an active universe." The infant mainly *receives,* of course, but if he develops properly, the inward, creative contribution will steadily grow in significance.[2]

As the child advances his body seeks expression in "glad animal movements" and his senses expand with a fresh vitality, unrigidified by the "frost" of "custom." Nothing clouds these early sensations, because the mind interposes no false barriers between itself and its objects. This unreflective keenness of his early sensibilities is very skillfully conveyed by Wordsworth.

But there is another aspect of the poet's childhood. This is its "all-soulness":

Fallings from us, vanishings;
Blank misgivings of a Creature
Moving about in worlds not realized.

Wordsworth remarked on several occasions that there were times in his childhood when he lost himself in an "abyss of idealism," intervals when he was sure only of his own mind; "everything else fell away and vanished into thought."[3] So complete was his abstraction that he had to clench the top bar of a gate or tightly grasp a tree in order to recall himself to reality.

This profundity of idealism was manifested in sensation as well as in withdrawal from external stimulation. Hence Wordsworth emphasizes the "glory and dream" of childhood. The poet felt that his mind's inward contribution to beauty was most patent (although not most deep) during his earliest years. The objects of sense were clothed with a strange radiance because sensations were informed by the mind. The "celestial" brightness of impressions was due to their immersion in the "clouds of glory" which the mind trails with it from its "home." All that he beheld shone in pure light, because his spirit shed its own radiance over the apparitions of sense.

The child, in its perception of the "visionary gleam," penetrates into the eternal order. He does this by intuiting a beauty simple and calm and happy, the highest pledge of the mind's kinship with God. For this temporal beauty is heightened by its participation in eternal beauty, which the mind brings "from afar." It is precisely because the child thus sees with the eye of the soul that he can be entitled the "best Philosopher." He deserves this title only in a restricted sense: not by virtue of intellectual penetration, but by reason of those powers which infect sensation with absolute beauty, a possession inborn.[4]

In the great *Ode* the child's idealistic spirit is represented as investing objects of sense with this "dreamlike vividness and splendour." The other poetry of Wordsworth will provide similar evidence. Something of the boy's inward life, for example, is captured in the famous account of the stealing of the boat, which made his brain "for many days" work "with a dim and undetermined sense of unknown modes of being."[5] Also in a poem composed in 1818, Wordsworth tells of a mood then rare but common in childhood—a sublime transport, a pure love, a supreme peace, a solemn harmony, a wonderful radiance, an exquisitely clear vision. It seems to him a second birth:

> Such hues from their celestial Urn
> Were wont to stream before mine eye,
> Where'er it wandered in the morn
> Of blissful infancy.[6]

We thus have abundant record of the mind informing the senses and shedding a glory from its mystical intuitions. Wordsworth portrays childhood not as the period of sensation merely, but as the joyous period in which the spirit had its internal prospects and its immortal light. Though the body was the focus of being, the mind might either dwell in abstraction or clothe the external world with the "glory and freshness of a dream."

II. Boyhood: The Stage of Emotion

The chief contrast between the first period and the second is to be found in the emergence of self-consciousness. The child's sensations are often bathed in his own idealism, but the inner brightness is objectified, attached to the external world. (This is not true of the states of abstraction, but these are only occasional). In boyhood, on the contrary, the poet awakens to a sense of the independence and creativeness of the mind.[7]

The transition to the second stage may conveniently be placed at ten years, in accordance with Wordsworth's suggestion:

> Twice five years
> Or less I might have seen, when first my mind
> With conscious pleasure opened to the charm
> Of words in tuneful order, found them sweet
> For their own *sakes,* a passion, and a power.[8]

Thus at this time he had adopted a more conscious attitude toward his creative faculties. He lived in a "delicious world of poesy," where "images, and sentiments, and words" "kept holiday."[9] Although at first his "intercourse with beauty" was "unconscious," he was more sensitive to nature and was less absorbed in mere "animal movements."[10]

This broadening of his awareness was not characterized by any break with the spirituality of childhood. He thus writes of the period of his early school days between his tenth and his seventeenth years:

> But let this
> Be not forgotten, that I still retained
> My first creative sensibility;
> That by the regular action of the world
> My soul was unsubdued. A plastic power
> Abode with me; a forming hand, at times
> Rebellious, acting in a devious mood;
> A local spirit of his own, at war
> With general tendency, but, for the most,
> Subservient strictly to external things
> With which it communed. An auxiliar light
> Came from my mind, which on the setting sun
> Bestowed new splendour; the melodious birds,
> The fluttering breezes, fountains that run on
> Murmuring so sweetly in themselves, obeyed
> A like dominion, and the midnight storm
> Grew darker in the presence of my eye.[11]

Sometimes the imaginative remoulding of experience passed over into moments of a distinctly mystical quality.

Another indication of his religious susceptibility was his frequent experience throughout boyhood of the emotions of fear and awe.[12]

III. YOUTH: THE STAGE OF FANCY

Between the second and third stage there is no sharp cleavage. Nevertheless Wordsworth does mention his seventeenth year as marking the point at which fancy began to dominate his outlook.[13] During the early ripening of his genius, his spirit expressed itself in the less profound operations of the poetic faculty. The trouble at this stage is that he had not learned

> . . .from. . .timely exercise to keep
> In wholesome separation the two natures,
> The one that feels, the other that observes.[14]

He was frequently guilty, therefore, of the pathetic fallacy, transferring to "unorganic natures" his own enjoyments. With joy in his own heart, he freely projected joy into the outer world. This play of fancy sometimes took other immature forms: "the yew tree had its ghost"; the forlorn widow drenched "the turf with never-ending tears"; the sunlight on a wet rock was a "burnished silver shield suspended over a knight's tomb."[15]

But fancy, enforced by a deeper imaginative insight, sometimes succeeded in attaining to a plane of vision which was highly significant to the developing Wordsworth:

> To every natural form, rock, fruit or flower,
> Even the loose stones that cover the high-way,
> I gave a moral life: I saw them feel,
> Or linked them to some feeling: the great mass
> Lay bedded in a quickening soul, and all
> That I beheld respired with inward meaning.[16]

This conception of reality was still crude; the youth forced nature to "put on" a "daily face" corresponding to some "transitory passion," and impressed his own moral life upon rocks and flowers and "every natural form." Hence he made his own world, a world that only lived for him and for God who pierces into the heart; but nevertheless a world that was fit subject for "heroic argument," because it represented an approach to a true and noble view of reality. This "eminence" of imagination was the "glory" of his youth, by means of which he mounted to "community with highest truth."[17]

It was in this period, after his first year in Cambridge, that the ever-memorable state of exaltation flooded his consciousness when he became a "dedicated spirit."[18] Also during this summer vacation he enjoyed an additional insight into the "life of things":

> Gently did my soul
> Put off her veil, and, self-transmuted, stood
> Naked, as in the presence of her God.[19]

Out of an experience that at least bordered on the mystical, a philosophy emerged that was distinctly un-naturalistic. Once more there was an attempt to rationalize the occurrence, but we miss the suggestion of immaturity:

> —Of that external scene which round me lay,
> Little, in this abstraction, did I see;
> Remembered less; but I had inward hopes
> And swellings of the spirit, was rapt and soothed,
> Conversed with promises, had glimmering views
> How life pervades the undecaying mind;
> How the immortal soul with God-like power
> Informs, creates, and thaws the deepest sleep
> That time can lay upon her.

The soul, Wordsworth announces, is essentially eternal and triumphs over the temporal order. It is this immortal soul which "informs" and "creates"; eternal forces operate within the mind.

These glimmering views were certain to work a change in the youth's outlook. Until now nature had been first and man had been second in his regard. But during the period of his early sojourn at Cambridge, his sympathies gradually shifted:

> Then rose
> Man, inwardly contemplated, and present
> In my own being, to a loftier height;
> As of all visible natures crown.[20]

If this state of mind had continued, he would soon have plunged into what would have approximated the fifth stage, although certain important values would have been lacking if the fourth period had been omitted. He had already left mere fancy far behind, and was ready to lift man to a primary place in his affections.

But there were intervals of retrogression before and after the profitable summer vacation. At Cambridge he found himself an "idler among academic bowers"; his attention became absorbed with "little bustling passions" and the "vice and folly" thrust upon his view. During this period his inward life declined; "imagination slept," although "not utterly." From the "timid course" of "scholastic studies" he turned " to travel with the shoal of. . .unthinking natures," and came under the sway of a friend, who has not yet been identified.[21] The effect of the companionship was to encourage "a treasonable growth of indecisive judgments." This impairment of "the mind's simplicity" was the beginning of a change to the next period in Wordsworth's life. The alteration, it should be remarked, was considered by the mature poet, no advance but a positive decline.[22]

At times the higher life flashed back into consciousness. A notable instance is the soaring of Wordsworth's imagination during his climb over the Alps with a friend, Robert Jones. The passage is familiar, but so magnificent that it can be read anew with pleasure:

> The immeasureable height
> Of woods decaying, never to be decayed,
> The stationary blasts of waterfalls,
> And in the narrow rent at every turn
> Winds thwarting winds, bewildered and forlorn,
> The torrents shooting from the clear blue sky,
> The rocks that muttered close upon our ears,
> Black drizzling crags that spake by the way-side
> As if a voice were in them, the sick sight
> And giddy prospect of the raving stream,
> The unfettered clouds and region of the Heavens,
> Were all like workings of one mind, the features
> Of the same face, blossoms upon one tree;
> Characters of the great Apocalypse,
> The types and symbols of Eternity,
> Of first, and last, and midst, and without end.[23]

The experience is recorded in the very language of a monistic idealism, the philosophy upon which transcendentalism is usually based. The last line defines the timelessness and infinity of the Absolute Mind.

On this same trip the two friends came into contact with the rising tide of the French Revolution, which was soon to sweep the poet into a new period in his development.

IV. EARLY MANHOOD: THE STAGE OF REASON AS A FACULTY OF JUDGMENT

By the age of twenty-two Wordsworth had reached a state in which man was foremost in his affections.[24] The transition to this period had been prepared from early childhood, but the sympathy for man's welfare was first blown into flames by the French Revolution. In 1792 he was in Blois, absorbed in converse with Michel Beaupuy, and by October of the same year he was in Paris, on the point of offering himself as a leader to the Girondists. The whirl of events and his own romance thrust nature into the background of his mind. The phases of Wordsworth's development which followed have been so fully dealt with by Harper and others, that I can omit a discussion of many aspects.

For a time after his return to England his mind was seized by rationalism, which at last culminated in devotion to abstract Godwinism. During this latter phase, he was "a Bigot to a new Idolatry," disposed to "unsoul. . .by syllogistic words. . .those mys-

teries of passion" which make "one brotherhood of all the human
race."[25] His mind was possessed by the faculty of analysis and
judgment, which must be classed as not inglorious, but as inferior
to the higher type of reason:

> There comes (if need be now to speak of this
> After such long detail of our mistakes)
> There comes a time when Reason, not the grand
> And simple Reason, but that humbler power
> Which carries on its no inglorious work
> By logic and minute analysis
> Is of all Idols that which pleases most
> The growing mind. A Trifler would he be
> Who on the obvious benefits should dwell
> That rise out of this process; but to speak
> Of all the narrow estimates of things
> Which hence originate were a worthy theme
> For philosophic Verse; suffice it here
> To hint that danger cannot but attend
> Upon a Function rather proud to be
> The enemy of falsehood, than the friend
> Of truth, to sit in judgment than to feel.[26]

The distinction that Wordsworth makes between the two types of
reason is important for the understanding of his thought. Just as
fancy, an inferior faculty of the poetic spirit, precedes imagination
in order of mental evolution, so also mere logical reason, a lower
faculty of the intellect, appears in advance of the synthetic reason,
which integrates thought and feeling. The contrast between these
two types of reason serves to differentiate this transitional phase,
when thought worked at variance with feeling, from what I have
termed the fifth stage.

The result of this licentiousness of the purely logical intellect
was nothing less than a withering of the imaginative life. Wordsworth carried the spirit of judgment into the midst of all his perceptions: "giving way to a comparison of scene with scene"; "dis-
liking here, and there liking" according to "rules of mimic art";
"roaming from hill to hill, from rock to rock," craving "combinations of new forms"; until his intellect suppressed his deeper feelings, but left his "bodily eye" unfettered.[27]

A number of critics have supposed that the resultant "absolute
dominion" of sensation applies to the period of youth and fancy,
when the mind was still very undeveloped. Instead, this state com-

mences subsequent to Wordsworth's return from France, a whole year after the age of reason had set in. Its initial phases are described in *Tintern Abbey;* during the earlier visit to the Wye in 1793, the poet's delight in "colours and forms" needed no "remoter charm, by thought supplied, nor any interest unborrowed from the eye." As the months went by, this sensationism progressed, until at the time of the moral crisis of 1795, the personality was reft in a "twofold frame of body and of mind."[28] Thus the clearest expression in Wordsworth of a surrender to sensation refers to a period when devotion to man and logic had brought on his "soul's last and lowest ebb."[29]

We must not suppose, however, that Wordsworth discards analytical reasoning. He is simply tracing the evolution of a mind which fights its way through incomplete loyalties to a rich and integral personality. The faculty of judgment and comparison, like the analogous gift of fancy, is an indispensable but subordinate constituent of the good life. It is below the synthetic reason because it introduces, when in command, a division into consciousness; for it becomes "sequestered" from the feelings and the imagination. After the same fashion, the "bodily eye" is to be subordinated to the "intellectual eye," because the latter eliminates the "twofold frame" of the divided personality.[30]

V. Maturity: The Stage of Imagination and the Grand and Simple Reason

Under the influence of Coleridge and Dorothy, and aided by his own inherent soundness of mind, Wordsworth finally emerged from his moral depression. This restoration brought with it a return of the experiences that he had known in his early days at Cambridge. He began to realize once more the "serene and blessed moods."

The way he interpreted these renewed experiences is indicated by a fragment of poetry published for the first time in the variorum edition of *The Prelude.* These lines are taken from a manuscript notebook filled with an early version of *Peter Bell* and various fragments from other poems. Upon the basis of internal evidence afforded by the notebook, Mr. de Selincourt decides that these lines were probably written between the summer of 1798 and February, 1800:

> I seemed to learn [   ][31]
> That what we see of forms and images
> Which float along our minds, and what we feel
> Of active or recognizable thought,
> Prospectiveness, or intellect, or will,
> Not only is not worthy to be deemed
> Our being, to be prized as what we are,
> But is the very littleness of life.
> Such consciousness I deem but accidents,
> Relapses from the one interior life
> That lives in all things, sacred from the touch
> Of that false secondary power by which
> In weakness we create distinctions, then
> Believe that all our puny boundaries are things
> Which we perceive and not which we have made;
> —In which all beings live with god, themselves
> Are god, Existing in the mighty whole,
> As indistinguishable as the cloudless East
> At noon is from the cloudless west, when all
> The hemisphere is one cerulean blue.[32]

This fragment proves that Wordsworth was very deeply affected by a mystical conception of reality. Forms and images represent the very littleness of life; and intellective processes are mere relapses from the unitary life in which all beings share. All our puny boundaries are man-made; the true reality is the ineffable unity. The *"one interior* life lives *in* all things"; therefore sensations, with their report of the external world, are mere "accidents" in comparison with the inward sense that we are god. Thus Wordsworth presents a sweeping denial of the senses and the reason, and an assertion of a completely mystical philosophy.

It may be objected that the poet did not finally include this manuscript fragment in *The Prelude,* and that the thought must have represented, therefore, an aberration which was rejected in a more reasonable mood. Fortunately we can give this objection its proper weight.

We have reason to hope that the passage in *The Prelude* which reproduces four of the lines might furnish some indication why the substance of the entire first draft was not incorporated. Turning to this passage, we find a tribute to Coleridge which was quoted in our first chapter. The two lines immediately following the lines reproduced are these:

> To thee, unblinded by these formal arts,
> The unity of all hath been revealed.[33]

It appears from this statement that Wordsworth agreed with Coleridge in asserting the unity that he so positively affirmed in the fragment. This declaration, however, is much more moderate and non-
committal than the lines which follow the denunciation of "the false
secondary power" in the first manuscript version. Why did the poet
thus temper his statement? We suspect that it was due to Coleridge's influence, because the entire passage as it appears in Book
II is concerned with Coleridge and his ideas. We therefore turn
to another passage which sums up Wordsworth's indebtedness to his
friend. Here we find a statement, also reproduced in our first chapter, describing the transition from pantheism to an immanent theism
whereby "God and Man" are "divided as they ought" and:

> Between them the great system of the world
> Where Man is sphered, and which God animates.[34]

Thus it becomes clearer than ever that Wordsworth had an early
period of mystical and radically pantheistic conviction, and that Coleridge finally converted him to a decided modification of this philosophy. This change in belief must be the explanation for Wordsworth's revisions of the sentiments contained in the manuscript fragment.

One must protest, however, against the view that the mystical
consciousness that surged up in Wordsworth's mind as a young
man did not have a very deep effect upon his experience.[35] Whenever he portrays these deeper moods his words quicken with heightened vitality. The fire of his imagination burns without quivering,
in a quiet, intense flame. It may be that we are here touching upon
the mystery of his genius, approaching the great "hiding-place" of
his power. In the following lines from *The Recluse,* written in 1800,
we are permitted to peer deep into his mind:

> Of ill-advised Ambition and of Pride
> I would stand clear, but yet to me I feel
> That an internal brightness is vouchsafed
> That must not die, that must not pass away.
> Possessions have I that are solely mine,
> Something within which yet is shared by none,
> Not even the nearest to me and most dear,
> Something which power and effort may impart:
> I would impart it, I would spread it wide.[36]

What is this "internal brightness" which none other shares, not even the nearest to him and the dearest? Not mere sensitive acuteness to the external world, because he shared this with Dorothy:

> She gave me eyes, she gave me ears.[37]

Not simply philosophical insight, because he recognized Coleridge's pre-eminence in this respect. Not poetical genius, because this could never be transferred. It was, I think, nothing less than the deep pervasive joy that pulsed through his being as a result of the mystical intuitions that neither Dorothy, nor Coleridge, nor any of his friends, could quite share with him. The aspiration that troubled his dreams and irradiated his whole moral being, was to impart the vision which his lonely spirit had captured.

He had now attained a maturity of insight and a breadth of personality for which all his experience had prepared him. The excesses of fancy, sensationism, analytical reason, and mysticism, had been rooted out, but not before new values had been sown by each phase. The higher faculties of imagination and synthetic reason controlled the lower, but they did not substitute themselves in place of the inferior powers. There was no annihilation of the lesser faculties, no swamping out of fancy, analysis, and sensuousness, for this suppression would have deprived the greater functions of their support, dissipating them in a vacuous idealism. Instead there was complete representation of the several aspects of the personality— sense, emotion, reason, and spirit—of which the higher were not earth-spurning. Even though man was now primary in Wordsworth's regard, he was still "wedded to this goodly universe in love and holy passion." I have been presenting, to be sure, the ideal extension and correction of his real self; but to a remarkable degree he approximated this state in creation and practice. To do so was his greatest achievement, of which *Tintern Abbey,* the *Intimations Ode,* and *The Prelude* offer the record which will "look Time's leaguer down."[38]

This richness without confusion, this fullness of harmony, was altogether too rare and difficult to remain for long the organizing principle of Wordsworth's personality. One of the first constituents to drop out of his life was his semi-mystical experiences. At the age of about thirty or a few years later his trance-like moments seemed to have ceased. There is perhaps a suggestion of this change in *The Prelude:*

> The days gone by
> Return upon me almost from the dawn
> Of life: the hiding-places of man's power
> Open; I would approach them, but they close.
> I see by glimpses now; when age comes on,
> May scarcely see at all; and I would give,
> While yet we may, as far as words can give,
> Substance and life to what I feel.[39]

In the *Intimations of Immortality* he recognizes the departure of the raptures that he had known, but he takes comfort in the reflection that faith and thought can even more completely reconcile him to life than did his old intense experiences.

Probably one reason why he so emphasizes the role of memory in the poetry written in his maturity, is that he found that his ecstasy was departing or had already gone; and that the only way to secure values deep enough to take its place, was by the brooding processes of recollection which recreated a new mood somewhat like the first, or even richer and deeper than the old mood. Yet the conscious effort involved in remembrance was not permanently to sustain him in the highest realm of being.

We need not seek to trace the change in heart and mind which he underwent in later years. It will be enough to indicate a poem that records his alteration. In *Composed Upon an Evening of Extraordinary Beauty and Splendour,* written in 1819, Wordsworth describes the "fervent rapture" that suddenly visits him and recalls to his mind the glories of childhood. He then proceeds:

> This glimpse of glory, why renewed?
> Nay, rather speak with gratitude;
> For if a vestige of those gleams
> Survived, 'twas only in my dreams.
> Dread Power! whom peace and calmness serve
> No less than Nature's threatening voice,
> If aught unworthy be my choice,
> From Thee if I would swerve;
> Oh, let Thy grace remind me of the light
> Full early lost, and fruitlessly deplored;
> Which, at this moment, on my waking sight
> Appears to shine, by miracle restored;
> My soul, though yet confined to earth,
> Rejoices in a second birth!
> —'Tis past the visionary splendour fades;
> And night approaches with her shades.[40]

It becomes evident upon a careful reading of the poem that the "second birth" is simply the "glimpse of glory" that immediately departs. This rebirth is merely "the dower bestowed on this transcendent hour"; it is only the "visionary splendour" that "fades" while "night approaches with her shades." He "fruitlessly deplored" "the light full early lost," because he was powerless to regain the visionary gleam of that far off time, and not because (as one critic believes) Wordsworth considered "blissful infancy" the first stage in a necessary development to continuously better forms of mental life. By 1819 he had lost touch with the complete synthesis of manhood as well as the fervent raptures of childhood.

What I have tried to prove in this chapter may be summarized as follows: The reader may discover in Wordsworth's life five periods which severally represent the dominion of one or two major faculties of his mind: sensation, emotion, fancy, analytical reason, synthetic reason, and imagination. It should not be understood by this division that there are distinct stages or mental factors which must always be thought of as separate. What I have called the stage of sensation is very idealistic; the stage of emotion is thoughtful and creative; imagination almost dominates the stage of fancy; the period of analytical reason brings an interval of intense hunger and passion; the stage of imagination and the "grand" reason is often merely fanciful, and frequently logical in the narrow sense: in other words, the five-fold division is an abstraction employed for the sake of a fuller understanding.

By this approach I have sought to make one fact clear: Wordsworth's mind was not a mechanical structure in which one function excluded another; it was a vital evolution in which the early processes of growth were incorporated into the completed economy. The fundamental conception in his ethical theory is the relational and conservative nature of value. The fruits of earlier development are focussed in the mature mind, "gathered and contained there like rays in a prism"; when thus captured they saturate the entire spirit with their reciprocal light. We discover a hierarchy of values, to be sure, but not the benevolent tyranny of reason to be found in rationalistic ethics; the higher state protects the lower because it is constituted thereof. Thus a great inwardness is achieved without the sacrifice of a shrewd outwardness; the poet remains "true to the kindred points of heaven and home."

III

TRANSCENDENTALISM

Transcendental knowledge is that by which we endeavor to climb above
our experience into its sources by an analysis of our intellectual faculties,
still however standing as it were on the shoulders of our experience, in
order to reach at truths which are above experience.

COLERIDGE[1]

I

We approach now what seems to be the great paradox of
Wordsworth, his simultaneous attachment to the senses and to an
unsensationistic theory of the mind. Some critics have been so impressed by the poet's tenacious hold upon the visible world that they
have denied his belief in ideas underivative from experience. This
view is plausible in the light of much of the evidence that we examined in the last chapter. We found that the poet conceived of life
as evolving from lowest to highest, from mere physical movement to
the noblest exercise of reason and imagination. We discovered that
the principle of this evolution was the conservation of values: the
grosser mental processes fed the purer; every lower faculty sustained
the higher powers; the genuine values in each stage of development
found articulation in the final organization of the personality. This
account of the growth of personality might lead us to expect that
the supersensuous is merely a refinement of the sensuous, that sense
is translated into soul without change of essence. Yet we find in
Wordsworth a good many passages that conflict with a sensationistic
account of mental life. Any satisfactory interpretation of the poet's
thought must explain this seeming contradiction between his natur-
ism and his transcendentalism.

By transcendentalism we are to understand the doctrine that
some ideas or forms of thought do not derive from experience but
from the constitution of the mind or from a supra-personal agency
communicating its message to consciousness (as in the case of Emer-
son's "oversoul"). We are not to confuse this concept with the
belief that sometimes passes under the same name, that God "transcends" man and nature, existing over and apart from them. The
meaning adopted in this chapter is entirely consistent with pantheism.
Another possible mistake would be to identify the doctrine with the
movement in nineteenth century thought known as transcendentalism. We need a wider significance, which embraces Plato's "forms,"
Descartes' "innate ideas," and Kant's "categories."

27

It would also be wrong to think of transcendentalism as inconsistent with a high evaluation of experience. The meaning will be clarified by reference to the Platonic form of the theory, which has hearkened to the "long and difficult language of facts."[2] According to Plato, experience serves to make explicit that which is already implicit within the mind. We have ideals or standards of the true, the good, the beautiful, and nothing in nature entirely corresponds to them. The circle of the mathematician, for example, has a perfection that no real circle attains; his lines have no breadth; his points have no dimensions; his cones no deviations from accuracy; all his reasoning concerns ideal points, lines, surfaces, solids. He is dealing with things that have never been seen or in any way known to sense. But the approximations of nature must be presented to the mind before the ideal mathematical forms may be conceived. In the same way, men have other unlimited, unempirical notions: for example, the idea of a "beauty absolute, separate, simple, and everlasting," which is not to be found "in animal, or in heaven, or in earth, or in any other place."[3] But before any of these innate forms or ideas, these universal concepts or principles, can be aroused in the mind, sense must present their semblances to the intellect. In this evoking of the forms and standards, there is no question of processes entirely independent of experience. What occurs according to Platonism is made fairly clear by Henry More, who thus explains the meaning which he attaches to "innate ideas":

> I do not mean that there is a certain number of ideas flaring and shining to the animadversive faculty, like so many torches or starres in the firmament to our outward sight,. . .but I understand thereby an active sagacity in the soul, . . . whereby some small businesses being hinted unto her, she runs out presently into a more clear and large conception.[4]

With somewhat tedious explicitness I have sought to make very clear the nature of the issue at stake. It cannot be proved that Wordsworth rejected the belief in innate or transcendental factors in knowledge, if it can merely be shown that he believed the mind dependent upon experience. Not only Plato but Kant and Coleridge believed that stimulus brings into play the transcendental factors in knowledge. To be a transcendentalist, Wordsworth had no need to follow any such extremist as Malebranche, who thought that truth comes not by any searching of the outer world, nor by any groping and development, but by a simple process of introspection.

II

An interesting illustration of the poet's conviction that sense arouses transcendental ideas may be found in his account of crossing the Alps with Robert Jones. The two young vacationers from Cambridge were astonished when they discovered that they had actually passed over the summit of the mountains. In a very Platonic spirit Wordsworth explains their feelings by suggesting that the mind approaches nature with ideal norms and standards to which outer things imperfectly correspond. Thus there is evidence in the workings of man's consciousness that

> Our destiny, our being's heart and home,
> Is with infinitude, and only there.[5]

The poet therefore feels that man's primary allegiance is with the unbounded, the eternal.

A passage in Book V of *The Prelude* indicates exactly the same conception of the co-working of the senses and the intuitive faculties. The child's imagination is represented as seizing with avidity upon the books of "dreamers" and of "forgers of lawless tales." This hunger is caused by the "dumb yearnings" and "hidden appetites" that characterize childhood. The intensity of the inward urge is ground for profound hope:

> Our childhood sits,
> Our simple childhood, sits upon a throne
> That hath more power than all the elements.
> I guess not what this tells of Being past,
> Nor what it augurs of the life to come.[6]

The passage represents excellent Platonic doctrine. The soul, even of a child, has immortal longings and ideal standards. These hunger for the right sense stimulation to evoke them, but they tell "of Being past" and "of the life to come" because they so far transcend the world of experience. Pre-existence and immortality are inferred because the mind thus inwardly pricked on, is "unwilling to forego, confess, submit, uneasy, and unsettled," and hence appears to belong to an infinite and eternal order.

In writing of the benefits derived from mathematics, Wordsworth again expresses himself after the Platonic mode. He considers the abstractions of "geometric science" as the finite "type" of the infinite thought:

> Yet from this source more frequently I drew
> A pleasure calm and deeper, a still sense
> Of permanent and universal sway
> And paramount endowment in the mind,
> An image not unworthy of the one
> Surpassing Life, which out of space and time,
> Nor touched by welterings of passion, is
> And hath the name of God.[7]

The Platonists have loved to rise in the same way from the thought of the pure forms of geometry, which resemble God's "ideas," to the conception of an ideal and timeless existence.[8]

III

In a section of the *Ode* which was probably written in 1802,[9] Wordsworth attributes the child's mystical intuitions to the presence of innate factors in knowledge. The soul does not come into the world in "utter nakedness"; it "cometh from afar" with its glory still trailing and never to depart wholly. It is possible to urge against this interpretation Wordsworth's comment that he never meant to inculcate a belief in a prior state of existence but employed the idea for its poetic effectiveness.[10] But does this note really dispose of the problem? The central meaning of the passage is not the idea of pre-existence but the thought that we come into the world with innate forms of thought which have been bestowed on us by God.

Nothing in the statement of Wordsworth would contradict this doctrine. Many men have believed in the doctrine of innate knowledge who have rejected the idea of pre-existence. We have no reason, therefore, to believe that the poet was indulging in a mere conceit when he wrote: ". . .trailing clouds of glory do we come." In Wordsworth's comment, moreover, the poet does not deny belief even in the Platonic theory of "reminiscence"; he merely says that he did not mean "to inculcate such a belief." This comment, written in Wordsworth's old age, after orthodoxy had gained control of his mind, contains the additional declaration:

> It (the theory of reminiscence) is far too shadowy a notion to be recommended to faith as more than an element in our instincts of immortality. But let us bear in mind that, though the idea is not advanced in Revelation, there is nothing there to contradict it, and the fall of man presents an analogy in its favor.

These words suggest that Wordsworth, even at this more pious period, was half-convinced of pre-existence. Perhaps no stronger belief could be safely attributed to Plato.

We cannot do better than remember Coleridge's interpretation of the poem:

> The Ode was intended for such readers only as had been accustomed to watch the flux and reflux of their inmost nature, to venture at times into the twilight realms of consciousness, and to feel a deep interest in modes of inmost being, to which they know that the *attributes of time and space are inapplicable and alien,* but which can yet not be conveyed, save in attributes of time and space. For such readers the sense is sufficiently plain, and they will be as little disposed to charge Mr. Wordsworth with believing the Platonic pre-existence in the ordinary interpretation of the words, as I am to believe that Plato himself ever meant or taught it![11]

This comment by the friend who knew Wordsworth's mind most intimately fully bears out the view that the *Ode* expresses transcendental doctrines. The author rejected the idea of pre-existence only in the ordinary meaning of the words, and he was writing about modes of inmost being, to which the attributes of time and space are inapplicable and alien, about those modes, in other words, which transcend sensory knowledge.

But even if we should decide that a portion of the *Ode* must be discounted because the poet did not believe in Platonic reminiscence, the meaning of what remains is proof enough for my contention. If a child in reading the "eternal deep, haunted forever by the eternal mind" attains to truth that makes him the "best" of philosophers, the truth must be, at least partially, intuitive; for older individuals have all the evidence of their wider experience and their much more advanced reason at their disposal, yet they are said to be far blinder than the child. Upon the basis of a philosophy quite untranscendentalistic one would expect increasing insight as the individual matures; yet Wordsworth announces that the contrary is too often the fact.

A poem written in 1806, "Yes, It Was the Mountain Echo," demonstrates Wordsworth's belief in intuition. The writer definitely and unambiguously states that we hear "voices of two different natures," and that one kind of voice comes from beyond this world and is the voice of God:

> Have not *we* too?—yes, we have
> Answers, and we know not whence;
> Echoes from beyond the grave,
> Recognized intelligence!

> Such rebounds our inward ear
> Catches sometimes from afar—
> Listen, ponder, hold them dear;
> For of God,—of God they are.

In interpreting this little poem as transcendentalist in sentiment, we surely pass beyond the realm of conjecture. These lines are incontrovertible proof that in 1806 Wordsworth did not accept the principle that all mental states originate solely in sensation or experience.

In 1807 Wordsworth published another such poem, which was composed in the previous year:

> Nor will I praise a cloud, however bright,
> Disparaging Man's gifts, and proper food.
> Grove, isle, with every shape of sky-built dome,
> Though clad in colours beautiful and pure,
> Find in the heart of man no natural home:
> The immortal mind craves objects that endure:
> These cleave to it; from these it cannot roam,
> Nor they from it: their fellowship is secure.[12]

In these words the poet announces that the mind is linked to eternal things, and that the transitory objects of sensation find in the heart of man no natural home. It was the voice from God to the inward ear that the Wordsworth of this time considered fundamentally important.[13]

IV

The foregoing interpretation is in harmony with that of Coleridge. We have already seen that he agreed with our reading of the *Intimations of Immortality.* Fortunately we also have evidence that applies to an earlier period than the date of the *Ode.* Coleridge records the plans for the "great philosophical poem," which was projected not long after the two poets became well acquainted. Our informant in *Table Talk* (July 21, 1832) declares:

I cannot help regretting that Wordsworth did not first publish his thirteen books on the growth of the individual mind—superior, as I used to think, upon the whole, to *The Excursion.* . . . Then the plan laid out, and, I believe partly suggested by me, was that Wordsworth should assume the station of a man in mental repose, one whose principles were made up, and so prepared to deliver upon authority a system of philosophy. He was to treat man as man,—a subject of eye, ear, touch, and taste, in contact with external nature, and informing the senses from the mind, and not compounding a mind out of the senses.

The mind is not formed out of sense because sensation requires a mind to register it: therefore the mind comes first, as "lord and master."[14]   Its innate properties may perhaps derive color from fleeting outward things, but neither being nor essence. Sense must be instead subservient to mind, receiving its impress, its forms and idealizations.   Such was the philosophy that was to be expressed in *The Prelude* and the poem to which it was to be the preface.

Fulfillment of this intention in respect to *The Prelude* is indicated by Coleridge's reception of the work.   In order to gauge the significance of his words we must remember that Wordsworth had addressed the composition to him.   On the title page of the manuscript version appeared the inscription, "POEM: Title not yet fixed upon by WILLIAM WORDSWORTH addressed to S. T. COLERIDGE."   Direct references within the body of the work indicate that Wordsworth kept his fellow-writer in mind. He would, therefore, have taken particular pains to convey his true meaning to Coleridge.   On January 7, 1807, Wordsworth finished reading *The Prelude* to his friend, who was free to ask questions and to discuss the philosophical import.   On the night when the reading was finished, Coleridge composed part of his poem, *To William Wordsworth,* which he soon thereafter completed.   In this composition he records the impression which *The Prelude* made upon his mind. Thus he summarizes a portion of Wordsworth's theme:

> Theme hard as high!
> Of smiles spontaneous, and mysterious fear
> (The first born they of Reason and twinbirth),
> Of tides obedient to external force,
> And currents self-determined, as might seem,
> Or by interior Power; of moments awful,
> Now in thy hidden life, and now abroad.[15]

These lines indicate that Coleridge understood *The Prelude* to set forth doctrine at variance with a naturalistic philosophy.   It is true that the phrase "currents self-determined" *might* be interpreted to mean that the mind carries on entirely upon its fund of memories without any fresh intervention from the senses.   But Coleridge suggests that these "currents" may only be an appearance; the real control is exercised by an "interior Power" which actually, and not seemingly, operates within the mind.   Therefore, this "Power" is not only different from "external force," but is different from currents self-determined; it is supra-personal, transcendental, the voice from

God. Thus Coleridge regarded *The Prelude* as a work quite opposed to the main doctrine of a sensationistic philosophy. That he misunderstood his fellow poet in this respect is incredible, because there existed every desire and opportunity to avoid misapprehension.

An indication of Wordsworth's state of mind at the time of writing the later portions of *The Excursion,* is afforded by Coleridge's comments. In 1815 Coleridge was a transcendentalist and quite orthodox. Yet he accepted the newly published poem as a body of truisms. On April 3, 1815, he wrote to Lady Beaumont:

> As proofs met me in every part of "The Excursion" that the poet's genius had not flagged, I have sometimes fancied that, having by the conjoint operation of his own experiences, feelings, and reason, *himself* convinced *himself* of truths, which the generality of persons have either taken for granted from their infancy, or, at least, adopted in early life, he has attached all their own depth and weight to doctrines and words, which come almost as truisms or commonplaces to others.[16]

On May 30, Coleridge wrote to Wordsworth, expressing his regret and surprise that *The Excursion* did not contain a specific attack against Locke and the associationists:

> I supposed you first to have meditated the faculties of man in the abstract, in their correspondence with his sphere of action, and first in the feeling, touch, and taste, then in the eye, and last in the ear,—to have laid a solid and immovable foundation for the edifice by removing the sandy sophisms of Locke, and the mechanic dogmatists, and demonstrating that the senses were living growths and developments of the mind and spirit, in a much juster as well as higher sense, than the mind can be said to be formed out of the senses.[17]

Until 1810 Coleridge kept in fairly close communication with Wordsworth. After the quarrel of 1810, the association was less frequent, but there were intimate intermediaries like Lamb and Henry Crabb Robinson; so it is improbable that Coleridge was unacquainted with Wordsworth's philosophical outlook. In supposing, therefore, that Wordsworth would launch a definite and vigorous attack against Lockian philosophy, he must not have been guided by a mere surmise. He must have known Wordsworth's state of mind, and must have reared his expectations upon this knowledge. The letter to Lady Beaumont proves that at least he did not regard the teaching of *The Excursion* as reprehensible. He was simply disappointed that Wordsworth's anti-Lockianism did not find a more fully elaborated expression.

In the light of this cumulative evidence from Coleridge and Wordsworth the presence of transcendentalism in the poetry is beyond serious dispute.

V

I shall now point out the nature of the forces that Wordsworth recognized as intuitive or transcendental. We may conveniently class these as emotional, moral, intellectual, and aesthetic.

Among the emotional factors must be counted joy and love. These feelings do not originate solely in mere outward impressions; they spring from the deepest inward sources. In the last book of *The Prelude* the author imbeds love, as well as imagination, within the "mighty mind. . .that feeds upon infinity" and

> . . .is exalted by an underpresence,
> The sense of God, or whatsoe'er is dim
> Or vast in its own being.[18]

This deepest love is the essence and foundation of life: "for here do we begin and end," from here "all grandeur comes, all truth and beauty." It is possible to believe, of course, that Wordsworth meant to equate the underpresence with the impressions gained wholly from the senses, but the language urges a different meaning. Likewise it is conceivable that the poet was speaking loosely when he celebrates a love which is more than human, a "divine" love, which proceeds from the brooding soul of man.[19] The safest interpretation is that he was speaking literally, that he genuinely conceived of the profoundest love as welling up from the underpresence of God, from the "soul divine which we participate."[20]

Wordsworth identified the highest human joy with the "serene and blessed mood," the "deep power of joy," felt by minds that are "truly from the Deity":

> the highest bliss
> That can be known is theirs, the consciousness
> Of whom they are habitually infused
> Through every image, and through every thought,
> And all impressions.[21]

How can we account for this "highest bliss" unless "the consciousness" means realization of their "sublime dependence" upon God. The unity "in which all beings live with god, themselves are god" no longer received full credence, but the most intense joy might still be felt through inmost participation in the divine life. At a considerably later time, to be sure, Wordsworth abandoned this faith in favor of the doctrine of grace, which is the orthodox equivalent of transcendentalism.

There can be little question, in face of the complete evidence, that Wordsworth believed morality rested upon a transcendental foundation. A passage in *The Convention of Cintra* indicates his sympathy for Old England, when Hooker, Jeremy Taylor, John Milton, and the Cambridge Platonists were influential, before the time of the empirical ethics of the eighteenth century and the utilitarianism of his own day. The poet's open hostility to the "Experimental Philosophy" is recorded, and the "dictates of paramount and infallible Conscience" are contrasted with the "calculations of presumptuous expediency."[22] We surely will not confuse "infallible dictates" with the often fallible insight of experience.

The poetry lends support to the passage from *The Convention of Cintra*. In a section of *The Prelude*, Wordsworth expresses the same point of view as Kant, that the best and the worst, the highest and the lowest, the peasant and the philosopher, have the same power of arriving at valid moral judgments; because all are gifted with

> One sense for moral judgments, as one eye
> For the sun's light.

When strongly breathed upon by the sense of this unity, the soul feels

> . . . whence she is
> And passing through all Nature rests with god.[23]

In the *Ode to Duty* Wordsworth again bows to an absolute moral standard. In the next to the last stanza he asserts that duty wears "the Godhead's most benignant grace" and controls, not only the human mind, but the flowers, the stars, and "the most ancient heavens." Thus it clearly springs from a wider order of reality than human experience.[24] Our moral standards are not communicated to us through the senses, but by an "abstract intelligence" which is non-spatial and timeless.[25] Therefore we should yield "entire submission to the law of conscience" which is "God's most intimate presence in the soul."[26] This view, however, may not have been held before 1804, for the *Ode to Duty* suggests that Wordsworth's attitude towards the whole problem of morality had recently altered.

The impression of some critics that the poet never held to a transcendental theory of morality, no doubt arises from the tendency of all his thought to make the higher states include the lower. These scholars are quite right when they suppose that the poet hearkened to the voice of experience. But he would supplement this voice by another; he believed that men would attain to the highest morality through a co-working of prudence and conscience, of experiential foresight and transcendental wisdom.

If morality is intuitive in a measure, so must be reason, which establishes the moral laws:

> Reason and her pure
> Reflective acts to fix the moral law
> Deep in the conscience.[27]

The phrase, "pure reflective acts," is suggestive of the non-evidential character of the process. In another passage of *The Prelude*, Wordsworth identifies the profounder reason with the very base of human life.[28]

It is typical of his thought that he often does not clearly distinguish between reason and imagination; he refers to them as if they were two aspects of one faculty. The explanation is that he regarded both as the empirical manifestation of the divine and immortal part of man. When he spoke of either imagination or reason in its highest signification, he was touching upon the very root of life, which he identified with divine love:

> Thy love is human merely; this proceeds
> More from the brooding Soul, and is divine.

> This love more intellectual cannot be
> Without Imagination, which, in truth,
> Is but another name for absolute strength
> And clearest insight, amplitude of mind,
> And reason in her most exalted mood.
> This faculty hath been the moving soul
> Of our long labour: we have traced the stream
> From darkness, and the very place of birth
> In its blind cavern, whence is faintly heard
> The sound of waters; follow'd it to light
> And open day, accompanied its course
> Among the ways of Nature, afterwards
> Lost sight of it bewilder'd and engulph'd,
> Then given it greeting, as it rose once more
> With strength, reflecting in its solemn breast

> The works of man and face of human life,
> And lastly, from its progress have we drawn
> The feeling of life endless, the great thought
> By which we live, Infinity and God.
> Imagination having been our theme,
> So also hath that intellectual love,
> For they are each in each, and cannot stand
> Dividually.[29]

This passage is important for a number of reasons. It not only indicates that life is essentially one, so that love and reason and imagination are almost interchangeable terms, but it also states the main theme of *The Prelude,* which is no less than the tracing of this inward shaping force that constitutes the deep and immortal being of man.

Wordsworth is at a loss to describe this power, which from one point of view may best be called imagination. Since it is the faculty by which we commune with infinity, it transcends all our efforts to confine it to the limits of language:

> Imagination—here the Power so called
> Through sad incompetence of human speech,
> That awful Power arose from the mind's abyss
> Like an unfathered vapour that enwraps,
> At once, some lonely traveller. I was lost;
> Halted without an effort to break through;
> But to my conscious soul I now can say—
> 'I recognize thy glory:' in such strength
> Of usurpation, when the light of sense
> Goes out, but with a flash that has revealed
> The invisible world, doth greatness make abode,
> There harbours; whether we be young or old,
> Our destiny, our being's heart and home,
> Is with infinitude, and only there.[30]

I believe we will not read this passage aright unless we interpret the "mind's abyss" as the center of being, where we are in contact with God. This power, arising from its "blind cavern," works in and through sensation, thus informing sense by the immortal mind.[31]

VI

We can now summarize in a few words the philosophy that dominates Wordsworth's thought. The base of the world is God, from "whence our dignity originates."[32] The highest faculties, when pricked on by the senses, arise inwardly from this base. These powers or faculties not only give being to man, but also maintain an "ennobling interchange" with the outer world, which rests upon the same foundation and which calls them into play.   Since in Wordsworth's view the transcendental faculties seem thus always to implicate sensation or introspective experience, he appears to discard all "innate ideas" in the *strict* sense of the term.   He gives great weight to the sensory factors in knowledge, because he realizes "how exquisitely. . .the external World is fitted to the Mind."   In *Tintern Abbey* he even goes so far as to state that nature and the language of the sense is the soul of all his moral being.   By this he does not mean that there is nothing in the mind not derived from sensation; he simply affirms that the inward faculties must be aroused by the "speaking face of nature."[33]   The mightiest life is to be achieved by combining the empirical and transcendental factors into a most potent unity:

> and as it were
> Resolving into one great faculty
> Of being bodily eye and spiritual need,
> The converse which he holds is limitless;
> Not only with the firmament of thought,
> But nearer home he looks with the same eye
> Through the entire abyss of things.[34]

IV

THE VOICE OF EXPERIENCE

Love had he found in huts where poor men lie;
His daily teachers had been woods and rills,
The silence that is in the starry sky,
The sleep that is among the lonely hills.[1]

I

We have seen that Wordsworth recognized "voices of two different natures," one of them received from experience, the other from inmost modes of being. These two voices are so intimately associated that the second follows from the first, like an echo "giving sound. . .for sound"; yet it would be wrong to confuse the two. Since we have already examined the inward voice, we have left to discuss the voice of experience and its reception into the mind.

Recognizing that sensation does play momentously upon the mind, Wordsworth was confronted with the problem of the reactions which follow. He early found in Hartleianism, as conveyed to him by Coleridge and independent study, an elaborate account of sensory stimulation and the consequent formation of ideas. Like Coleridge, he rejected Hartley's sensationism as an exclusive theory. But he found that the associational psychology could be applied to one side of mental life, and he partially accepted Hartley's analysis within these limits.[2]

Hartley maintained that association is a universal law of mental operations, as important to psychology as the law of gravitation is to physics. He reduced his basic thought to a single clear principle: sensations or ideas become associated when they appear in the mind "at the same Instant of Time, or in contiguous successive instants." Thus if I see a cat hissing at a dog, I shall be inclined to remember the dog when I again catch sight of the cat. All such associations may become increasingly complex: around the thought of the cat may collect many suggestions—milk, catnip, scratches, maternity, bad luck. In the case of highly "intellectual ideas," the elements that contribute to the associational clusters are often so numerous and so faded that the complex idea discovered in the mind may balk all attempt to analyse it. The idea of justice, for example, is such a composite, in which the ideas and feelings gained from a great range of experience have coalesced into a most abstract concept. We cannot trace back all the associated elements; but a strict associationist nevertheless believes that the conception of justice is formed after the same fashion as the notion of the cat.[3]

Wordsworth made a considerable use of the principle of association. By this means he explains, for example, how man became exalted in his boyish eyes, when he saw shepherds glorified by the deep radiance of the setting sun or silhouetted against the sky on the mountain height. He at first "looked at man through objects that were great or fair"; hence the human form was loved because it was to be seen on the glowing hills or along the winding streams; the sight of man evoked emotions derived from his environment. In the period of maturity the association was often reverse: the poet heard in nature the still sad music of humanity; the common haunts of the green earth were more dear for the sake of love and friendship. No other writer has expressed so frequently and so subtly this reciprocity of relationship, through which the love of man is ennobled and the sympathy with nature is intensified.

The associational psychology served partially to explain the interdependence that pervaded consciousness. Wordsworth could find little disconnection in the well-fashioned soul; every part of the mind seemed to implicate all the rest in itself. Relatedness bound his days each to each with natural piety. Also association created within the mind a body of sympathetic responses, so that each mental process was enriched by its affiliations; if one string of the soul was plucked, the other strings vibrated in unison. Wordsworth frequently illustrates the growth of these systems of relationships which involve each other in their interplay. He revealed, in particular, how nature intertwined for him

> The passions that build up our human soul;
> Not with the mean and vulgar works of man,
> But with high objects, with enduring things.[4]

When the mind became "a mansion for all lovely forms," life itself took on something of the integrality of a poem whose texture is interwoven by the ceaseless shuttle of syntax.

We should recognize, however, that Wordsworth penetrated through emotion to thought; and not *vice versa*. I mean that he had initially felt and lived the relations, and that he had subsequently utilized associationism to explain them. He had achieved in his own life an organic interfusion of elements; otherwise he would not have been attracted to Hartley's psychology. As soon as he found that

Hartleianism was inadequate to explain the facts of his experience, he leaped beyond it into supplementary or even contradictory notions. He modified Hartley's optimism, rejected his necessitarianism, overstepped his rationalism, abandoned his strict sensationism, put an entirely different evaluation upon the imagination, conceived of the mind as very active instead of relatively passive, and supplemented the principle of association with other theories which would explain the unity of the mind. Some of these deviations are so significant that we should not neglect to scrutinize them.

II

Wordsworth's account of the associational process is more modern than Hartley's. According to the prevalent theories of the eighteenth century, combinations never give birth to anything genuinely new: "the whole was supposed to be directly resolvable into its parts without remainder."[5] The notion of evolution in mental life was quite far from the thoughts of these early psychologists; they recognized the addition of new elements drawn from experience, but they did not discern that mental syntheses give rise to radically new content. Hartley adheres, for the most part, to this old mechanistic view of mental processes, rather than to the new vitalistic appreciation of the significance of fusions.[6]

Wordsworth consistently holds to the more advanced position. I do not mean that he enunciates the idea of creative synthesis in any overt or doctrinaire manner; I merely mean that he does see nature *en bloc,* each element transfused and modified by the atmosphere of the whole. This is the way his imagination works; his method as a poet separates him from the traditional psychologists, and this imaginative divergence is just as important as any intellectualistic distinction.

We might select many passages to illustrate his sense of a general tone and quality that emerges from a blending of the particulars in each synthesis. In the following, one notes that all the sounds are abstracted from their objects, and are fused into one song that seems the "natural produce of the air":

> Up the brook
> I roamed in the confusion of my heart,
> Alive to all things and forgetting all.
> At length I to a sudden turning came
> In this continuous glen, where down a rock

> The Stream, so ardent in its course before,
> Sent forth such sallies of glad sound, that all
> Which I till then had heard appeared the voice
> Of common pleasure: beast and birds, the lamb,
> The shepherd's dog, the linnet and the thrush,
> Vied with this waterfall, and made a song
> Which, while I listened, seemed like the wild growth
> Or like some natural produce of the air,
> That could not cease to be.[7]

There is more than a mere summation—there is a genuine merging that is not to be confused with a simple addition of sound.

Wordsworth's characteristic method is to abstract from each object its individuating characteristics, to emphasize its communal properties, and to almost lose it in the reciprocal glow. The cuckoo, for example, is "no bird, but an invisible thing, a voice, a mystery," which summons to the mind the visionary memories of childhood, and thus so interfuses the past with the present that the earth itself seems an "unsubstantial, faery place" composed like the bird of the stuff of phantoms. In the poem, *To A Highland Girl,* the maid, the grey rocks, the household lawn, the waterfall, the silent lake, the quiet road, and the half-veiled trees, "together. . .seem like something fashioned in a dream." In *Resolution and Independence,* the old Leechgatherer is "not all alive nor dead," and the huge stone to which he is compared "seems a thing endued with sense"; the environment thus assumes human characteristics, and the old man becomes very nearly elemental and sub-human. The result is a unity, an interfusion, and a visionary and dreamlike atmosphere. It is remarkable that the poet could achieve these syntheses within imagination, and at the same time convince the reader that he had kept his "eye on the object."

A passage from *The Prelude* is selected by Professor Whitehead as a clear expression of its author's "feeling for nature, as exhibiting entwined prehensive unities, each suffused with modal presences of others":[8]

> Ye Presences of Nature in the sky
> And on the earth! Ye Visions of the hills!
> And Souls of lonely places! can I think
> A vulgar hope was yours when ye employed
> Such ministry, when ye through many a year
> Haunting me thus among my boyish sports,
> On caves and trees, upon the woods and hills,
> Impressed upon all forms the characters
> Of danger or desire; and thus did make
> The surface of the universal earth
> With triumph and delight, with hope and fear,
> Work like a sea?[9]

In such a passage as this, Wordsworth outstrips even the more advanced psychologists in his own day. The significant fact is that the synthesis is not effected by the mind *after* sensation, but the sensations appear to enter into consciousness already synthesized.[10]

In a very important passage in the concluding book of *The Prelude,* the poet recognizes these two kinds of fusion, the one found in nature and the other created in the mind. He has been describing a climb to the summit of Snowdon:

> With forehead bent
> Earthward, as if in opposition set
> Against an enemy, I panted up
> With eager pace, and no less eager thoughts.
> Thus might we wear perhaps an hour away,
> Ascending at loose distance each from each,
> And I, as chanced, the foremost of the Band;
> When at my feet the ground appear'd to brighten,
> And with a step or two seem'd brighter still;
> Nor had I time to ask the cause of this,
> For instantly a Light upon the turf
> Fell like a flash: I looked about, and lo!
> The Moon stood naked in the Heavens, at height
> Immense above my head, and on the shore
> I found myself of a huge sea of mist,
> Which, meek and silent, rested at my feet:
> A hundred hills their dusky backs upheaved
> All over this still Ocean, and beyond,
> Far, far beyond, the vapours shot themselves,
> In headlands, tongues, and promonotory shapes,
> Into the Sea, the real Sea, that seem'd
> To dwindle, and give up its majesty,
> Usurp'd upon as far as sight could reach.
> Meanwhile, the Moon look'd down upon this shew

> In single glory, and we stood, the mist
> Touching our very feet; and from the shore
> At distance not the third part of a mile
> Was a blue chasm; a fracture in the vapour,
> A deep and gloomy breathing-place through which
> Mounted the roar of waters, torrents, streams
> Innumerable, roaring with one voice.
> The universal spectacle throughout
> Was shaped for admiration and delight,
> Grand in itself alone, but in that breach
> Through which the homeless voice of waters rose,
> That dark deep thoroughfare had Nature lodg'd
> The Soul, the Imagination of the whole.[11]

This grand prospect, with all its various constituents, had one soul, which was most nearly represented by the blue chasm through which rose the homeless voice of waters. The mention of "Imagination" is significant, because the poet is establishing a similarity between synthesis in nature and imaginative synthesis in man. The vision that rose before him on the mountain top was "the perfect image of a mighty Mind":

> above all
> One function of such mind had Nature there
> Exhibited by putting forth, and that
> With circumstance most awful and sublime,
> That domination which she oftentimes
> Exerts upon the outward face of things,
> So moulds them, and endues, abstracts, combines,
> Or by abrupt and unhabitual influence
> Doth make one object so impress itself
> Upon all others, and pervade them so
> That even the grossest minds must see and hear
> And cannot chuse but feel.[12]

In this passage Wordsworth presents his interpretation of imagination. It is not only a transcendental faculty, as we saw in the previous chapter, but it is essentially a creative one, because the syntheses which it effects give to the mind a wholly new reality.

This description of imagination will be found to agree with the poet's famous distinctions between fancy and imagination. Fancy is mechanical; imagination is creative and transcendental. Fancy combines without modifying; its associations are forced or superficial. Imagination alters by fusion; it unites objects that have real affinities for each other.

III

To complete the account of imagination, we must briefly consider the relation between its transcendental roots and its synthetic activities. Wordsworth nowhere gives a clear exposition of this relationship; and the following suggestions are therefore offered as merely inferential.

We can best understand the theory by discovering its point of departure from associationism. Association for Hartley is reduced to a single principle: the welding together of elements through contiguous occurrence.[13] In other words, all mental development is traced back to the *immediate* spatial and time relations between sensations and their copies. It is true that mental complexes, when once built up, furnish magnetic points to which new content may be attached, but only if the principle of contiguity permits. Thus Hartley most effectually eliminates as an operating factor in knowledge, the reference of the mind beyond its immediate state.

Kant objected to any such theory because it fails to account for the unity of consciousness. The mere principle of succession cannot explain even the simple ideas of succession:

> Now, when I draw a line in thought, or if I think the time from one noon to another, or if I only represent to myself a certain number, it is clear that I must first necessarily apprehend one of these manifold representations after another. If I were to lose from my thoughts what precedes, whether the first parts of a line or the antecedent portions of time, or the numerical unities representing one after the other, and if, while I proceed to what follows, I were unable to reproduce what came before, there would never be a complete representation, and none of the before-mentioned thoughts, not even the first and purest representations of space and time, could ever arise within us.[14]

Thus even these elementary forms of consciousness imply a "unity of apperception": we must first reproduce the images and ideas in memory; then whatever is remembered must be recognized as referring to the past, and this presupposes a self-consciousness which recognizes past impressions as inhering in one experience belonging to oneself. Finally, the contents of consciousness, present and past, must be so combined and unified that a synthesis of apprehension will be possible, whereby succession will be clearly grasped as such. All this implies a decided transcending of the single principle of association. It implies a unitary self-consciousness antecedent to the experience in question and rendering that experience possible.

Kant therefore found it necessary to supplement the idea of association with another principle: the transcendental activity of the imagination, which produces an "affinity of all appearances," a genuine cohesion in consciousness. It is this working of the imagination that comes to the aid of associational processes and that renders them possible.[15]

Here was the solution that Coleridge discovered when he sought in German philosophy for an escape from the perplexities that Hartleianism had brought to his mind. He seized eagerly upon the Kantian conception of imagination and made it the basis of his well-known distinction between fancy and imagination. The central point in Coleridge's distinction, in its metaphysical aspect, is that imagination in contrast to fancy, organizes sensation in accordance with the transcendental principles of reason. This is exactly what Kant refers to when he speaks of a "synthesis in imagination which is grounded *a priori* on rules."[16]

It would appear that Wordsworth, at work on his great philosophical poem, and already sure that imagination is the grand faculty of life, embraced the opportunity afforded by Coleridge's new ideas for rationalizing his own experience of the oneness of God and Man. He seized upon the idea of imagination as a transcendental force, giving unity to all life and binding man to God. But he was not content like Kant to suppose that all the main work of the imagination is done in the "darkness" from whence it emerges. Instead he conceived of imagination as emerging into the daylight and the common world of men. He went beyond Kant also in identifying the "blind cavern" of imagination with the "underpresence" from which wells up "the sense of God." Thus he gave to the transcendental imagination a decidedly religious coloring. There is a mysterious region which lies deeper than our ordinary experience, a realm of subconsciousness, from "whence we draw our power." In times of ecstasy we flood this sphere with light, and feel the interior life through which we are in contact with God. But even when man lacks this deeper vision, his imagination may be active, drawing from the infinite depths of being and communicating to life the oneness which resides at the source of power.

This interpretation would explain why Wordsworth, like Kant, regards imagination as closely bound to the higher reason.[17] It would also explain the several processes by which unity in the mind is achieved: association accounts for the linkage of ideas or sensations which occur together; the synthetic imagination produces the more complete fusions; the transcendental imagination lends to the mind an *a priori* unity and self-consciousness. Although it is impossible to say that Wordsworth anywhere states these conceptions, the concluding book of the 1805-1806 *Prelude* seems consonant with no other interpretation.

IV

The life of imagination for Wordsworth means the full and active operation of inward faculties, through which the mind builds up great things from least suggestions. Intellectual freedom and activity is everywhere stressed by the poet. One of the supreme articles of his thought, a supposition that underlies passage after passage, is simply this idea: if imagination is once active, if the mind informs the senses, then a genuine and imperishable increment of power is added to existence.[18]

It is true that the poet was for a time a believer in necessity or the absence of free will. One bit of evidence is the letter from Coleridge quoted in chapter I, but this letter demonstrates that by January, 1804, at the very latest, Wordsworth had abandoned his conviction. The only other indications, so far as I know, consist in the testimony of a few of his early poems and in his known adherence for a time to the necessitarianism of Godwin.[19] Hazlitt believed that Wordsworth was expressing his necessitarianism in the famous lines from *Tintern Abbey* :[20]

> A motion and a spirit, that impels
> All thinking things, all objects of all thought,
> And rolls through all things.

The essayist is probably right in this interpretation; but at least the forces that make for necessity are represented as dwelling *within* the mind and do not operate upon it from the outside alone. The entire passage from which these lines are quoted strongly suggests Spinoza; and Spinoza's determinism did not exclude the remarkable tribute in the *Ethic* to "the power of the intellect" and its capacity for achieving a kind of freedom.

We may surely say that the general tenor of Wordsworth's thought is quite opposed to necessitarianism. The case of Peter Bell informs us of the attitude of his creator:

> . . .Nature could not touch his heart
> By lovely forms, and silent weather,
> And tender sounds. . . .[21]

The trouble is that Peter's mind is filled with

> . . .all the unshaped half-human thoughts
> Which solitary Nature feeds. . .[22]

There must be a decided inward shaping and humanization of impressions before they can be made fruitful. Thus in this poem, first written in 1798 and later revised, the author insists upon inward creativeness, without which there can be no progression toward a higher personality. This is his consistent attitude and his recurrent theme.[23]

V

To summarize: Wordsworth by no means minimizes the report of the senses. He recognizes that a being in communion with natural beauty must necessarily become wiser and nobler. Yet this intimate communion requires for its establishment a free and active mind that vitalizes the processes of association through its inward contribution. The highest manifestation of this mental activity is the work of imagination, which flows from the divine and mysterious underpresence. In this deep subliminal region, and also in the conscious life of the imagination, the disparate elements of experience are grasped together and synthesized. Thus imagination produces a self-consciousness and a unitary life of the whole mind and spirit, whereas association could only introduce connections from next to next. When this integral mind seizes upon sensation, it fuses impressions into a new and irrefrangible unity. Yet consciousness does not always need to create these profounder syntheses; at times sensations enter into the mind in synthesized form, so that the observer immediately grasps more than individuals or their mere summation. Hence a significant correlation may be established between the ways of nature and the works of the mind.

V

THE EXTERNAL WORLD

In his poetry nothing in Nature is dead. Nature is synonymous with life. . . . To such a mind, we say—call it strength or weakness—if weakness assuredly a fortunate one—the visible and audible things of creation present, not symbols or curious emblems—which they have done at all times to those who have been gifted with the poetic faculty—but with revelations and quick insights into the life within us, the pledge of immortality.

CHARLES LAMB[1]

I

Two assumptions underlie Wordsworth's theory of the external world: that it is free and active, and that spiritual forces are at work. These unite in one idea, that outer things may be interpreted in idealistic terms.

In contrast to the notion of the world-machine which the eighteenth century conceived in the light of Newton's science, the poet formulates an account of existence in terms of freedom and activity everywhere to be found in nature. He applied the idea of freedom to least and greatest:

How does the Meadow-flower its bloom unfold?
Because the lovely little flower is free
Down to its root, and in that freedom, bold;
And so the grandeur of the Forest-tree
Comes not by casting in a formal mould,
But from its *own* divine vitality.[2]

As a complement to this attribution of creativeness and liberty to a little flower, *The Excursion* announces that there is a "freedom of the universe." An "active principle" is assigned to every form of being, so that no spot is insulated, and the free "soul of all the worlds" subsists in all things, in all natures.[3] Likewise in the first text of *The Prelude*, Wordsworth indicates his belief in an "active universe."[4]

If we now explore this inner life of nature as he conceives it, we find that one of its characteristics is its joy. Some of his remarks to this effect we may perhaps dismiss as metaphorical. The sonnet, "Brook Whose Society the Poet Seeks," announces that "unwearied Joy" has been bestowed upon the stream. "To the Daisy" speaks of the "cheerful Flower" as alert and gay. "I Wandered Lonely as a Cloud" presents the jocund daffodils that outdo the

sparkling waves in glee.   In all three poems, Wordsworth may be
only figurative in expression.   It may possibly be that he is not literal
in "Three Years She Grew in Sun and Shower," in which he represents Nature as moulding Lucy and imparting to her its own "vital
feelings of delight."   We are not so much inclined, on the other
hand, to dismiss as a mere play of fancy his statement in *The Pre-*
lude that nature "didst rejoice" with him, and the "soul of Nature"
"dost overflow with passion and with life."[5]   Nor can we easily
regard the following assertion as other than literal:

> Yet, whate'er enjoyments dwell
> In the impenetrable cell
> Of the silent heart which Nature
> Furnishes to every creature;
> Whatsoe'er we feel and know
> Too sedate for outward show,
> Such a light of gladness breaks,
> Pretty Kitten! from thy freaks.[6]

We have Wordsworth's own word that this section of the poem
should be taken in all seriousness.   Robinson recorded in his *Diary,*
September 10, 1816, that Wordsworth "quoted from 'The Kitten and
Falling Leaves,' to show that he had connected even the kitten with
the great, awful, and mysterious powers of nature."   No other
passage is relevant to the assertion.   This record in the *Diary* should
warn us that danger attends upon an interpretation of such declarations as mere examples of "charming fancy."[7]

The clearest statement to be found in Wordsworth of his belief
in nature's joyous life occurs in *Lines Written in Early Spring.*
Herein he states his "faith that every flower enjoys the air it
breathes."   In the birds and the budding twigs there is also en-
joyment:

> And I must think, do all I can,
> That there was pleasure there.

In *To My Sister,* the poet recognizes "a sense of joy" in nature, and
a "blessed power" that rolls through all things about us.   These
poems deserve a more absolute acceptance as a record of Wordsworth's thought than some critics have been inclined to give to them.

In such passages as this we discover the optimism of the poet.
He believed that nature imparted value to the "meanest of created
things":

> . . .a spirit and pulse of good,
> A life and soul, to every mode of being
> Inseparably linked.[8]

His optimism does not exclude frequent portrayal of human heart-break, for so complete is God's interpenetration with the world that even the most dire events subserve the grand plan of nature:

> But Thy most dreaded instrument,
> In working out a pure intent,
> Is Man—arrayed for mutual slaughter,
> —Yea, Carnage is thy daughter![9]

II

The Old Cumberland Beggar introduces another aspect of Wordsworth's conception of the natural world, the idea of the organic nature of value and existence. It is "Nature's law," he says, that "forms created the most vile and brute" should not "exist divorced from good." The life of the whole imparts a pulse of good to each fragment.[10] Value is not confined; it spreads outward until it affects the entire circumambient region:

> Whate'er exists hath properties that spread
> Beyond itself, communicating good,
> A simple blessing, or with evil mixed;
> Spirit that knows no insulated spot,
> No chasm, no solitude.[11]

It is because the poet recognizes the organic emanation and collection of value, that he protests vigorously against the false secondary power by which we multiply distinctions. It is because he feels that each small thing grasps together, within its inner being, the good that accumulates from the presence of surrounding things, that he maintains so deep a reverence for slight objects and that he affirms so often that "we murder to dissect."[12]

This vice of ever "dividing" mutilates reality, because one object impresses itself on all others and each part reflects its neighbors. Hence there are "Souls of lonely places" and "Visions of the Hills" and "Presences of Nature, in the sky and on the earth." This disposition to regard natural objects as interpenetrative appears in poem after poem. It constitutes much of the distinctiveness of "I Wandered Lonely as a Cloud." The *Lines Written in Early Spring* are pervaded with the sense of the suffused life of the whole. The spiritual unity of nature enters into the essence of *Nutting* and *Hart-leap Well*. A suggestion of life and interplay distinguishes many scattered lines:

> The Winds come to me from the fields of sleep,
>   And all the earth is gay
>
>   . . . .'mid all this mighty sum
> Of things for ever speaking.
>
> It is a beauteous evening, calm and free,
> The holy time is quiet as a Nun
> Breathless with adoration; the broad sun
> Is sinking down in its tranquillity;
> The gentleness of heaven broods o'er the Sea:
> Listen! the mighty Being is awake,
> And doth with his eternal motion make
> A sound like thunder—everlastingly.

Such examples show that there is no sharp cleavage between passages in which the poet definitely attributes "souls" or "presences" to nature, and passages in which he achieves a pervasive atmosphere that seems to express a totality of life.

It is interesting to find that man fits into the midst of these interplaying forces. A person's individuality seems almost lost amid its surroundings. In "Three Years She Grew in Sun and Shower" Lucy is taken up into the life of nature and incorporated with it. The same is true of Michael, the Leechgatherer, and the Solitary Reaper: they seem made all of a piece with the world around them, so that they almost have their being in the elemental or beauteous forms that pervade their domain.

Thus instead of viewing the external world as an abstract flux of isolated elements, Wordsworth regarded reality as infected throughout with relations and organic complexes, and as exhibiting concrete characteristics such as we find in life. Impressions thus possess a character which renders them fit to be absorbed into the unity of mental life. This resemblance between the inner and outer worlds lends a far deeper meaning to two of the poet's profound convictions: that the external world is exquisitely fitted to the mind, and that there is a mighty unity in which all things inhere.

III

From his own observation Wordsworth derived the chief basis for his view of nature. Gifted with a very extraordinary acuteness of perception, he was able to recognize that the prevalent analysis was false, that sensations actually come to us, not in any discrete form, but inextricably blended in solid mass.

He was also remarkably unaffected by the modifications in men's view of things introduced by our complex scientific civilization. His consciousness often functioned at a peculiarly undifferentiated level. To find a very similar mind in this respect, one has to journey beyond the inhibitions and sophistications imposed by the modern intelligence. All poets in some degree, to be sure, brush away the frost of custom, but not to the same degree or in the same way. Perhaps only among uncivilized people can one find the almost *sensuous* animism that reappears in Wordsworth. The perceptions of nature, as represented in early folk religions or among savages, are commonly fused with a spontaneous spiritism. The world *appeared* alive to these people and was thought to be so. Any reader of Wordsworth who is thoroughly immersed in the poetry must have noticed a similar ready animism.

These animistic touches are frequently presented in the form of simple perceptions:

> The Moon doth with delight
> Look round her when the heavens are bare.

When we read these lines in the *Intimations of Immortality* we do not find in them simply a play of fancy; they seem rather the report of something seen; they fit intimately into the earnest and idealistic mood of the poem. In the same way, we are almost credulous when we read:

> Unruffled doth the blue lake lie,
> The mountains looking on.[18]

The consciousness of life is so little differentiated from visual impressions that soul and sense quite intermingle.

IV

At times the animism becomes more absolute. Some of the early readings of *The Prelude* make use of the idea of "tutelary powers" which dwell in nature and guard over men. In a description of a country fair held at the base of Helvellyn, the author at first planned to introduce the following comment:

> Immense
> Is the Recess, the circumambient World
> Magnificent, by which they are embraced.
> They move about upon the soft green field:
> How little They, they and their doings seem,
> Their herds and flocks about them, they themselves,
> And all that they can further or obstruct!
> Through utter weakness pitiably dear
> As tender Infants are: and yet how great!
> For all things serve them, serve them for delight
> Or profit from the moment when the dawn
> Ah surely not without attendant gleams
> Of heart illumination strikes the sense
> With its first glistening on the silent rock
> Whose evening shadows led them to repose
> And doubt ye that these solitudes are paced
> By tutelary Powers more safely versed
> In weal and woe than aught that fabling Greece
> Invented, Spirits gentle and benign
> Who now perhaps from yon reposing cloud
> Look down upon them or frequent the ridge
> Of old Helvellyn listening to the stir
> That with this ancient festival returns
> To animate and chear their calm abode.[14]

Another remarkably animistic portion of *The Prelude* in its earliest
form, occurs in a passage that was designed to introduce the famous
boat stealing episode of the first book:

> The mind of man is fashioned and built up
> Even as a strain of music: I believe
> That there are Spirits which, when they would form
> A favored being, from his very dawn
> Of infancy do open out the clouds
> As at the touch of lightning, seeking him
> With gentle visitations, quiet Powers!
> Retired and seldom recognized, yet kind
> And to the very meanest not unknown.
> With me though rarely in my boyish days
> They communed; others too there are who use
> Yet haply aiming at the self-same end
> Severer interventions, ministry
> More palpable, and of their school was I.
> They guided me: one evening led by them
> I went alone into a Shepherd's Boat,
> A Skiff that to a Willow tree was tied
> Within a rocky Cave, its usual home.[15]

This first draft indicates how very animistic in inspiration certain now familiar passages must have been in their first conception.

One suspects that many sections of the poem were more naively spiritistic in their earliest design than in the form in which they have been preserved to us. We can only conjecture how the following statement might once have stood:

> A gracious spirit o'er this earth presides,
> And o'er the heart of man: invisibly
> It comes, to works of unreproved delight,
> And tendency benign, directing those
> Who care not, know not, think not what they do.[16]

Even if this reading represents the first draft, such a conception of a spirit's conscious ministrations seems to be merely a refinement of the early notion of tutelary powers. If we return to the passage in which the poet speaks of the "Souls of lonely places," we find that the language here too is not far removed from a frank animism. We have a variant reading in this instance that makes the interpretation almost indubitable:

> Ye Powers of earth, ye genii of the Springs
> And ye that have your voices in the clouds
> And ye that are familiars of the Lakes
> And standing pools, Ah, not for trivial ends
> Through snow and sunshine, through the sparkling plains
> Of moonlight frost and in the stormy day
> Did ye with such assiduous love pursue
> Your favorite and your joy.[17]

In the light of such unmitigated animism, we can attribute to some of Wordsworth's early poems a more literal signification than we have been wont to find in them. In *Nutting*, for example, the author may have meant quite unmetaphorically that there really is "a spirit in the woods." In "Three Years She Grew in Sun and Shower," the personification of Nature and the conscious overseeing power attributed to her, may not be fictitious from the point of view of the man who wrote the poem in 1799. Wordsworth might likewise have meant with entire literalness his explanation of the strange transformation around Hart-leap Well:

> "The Being that is in the clouds and air,
> That is in the green leaves among the groves,
> Maintains a deep and reverential care
> For the unoffending creatures whom he loves."[18]

Perhaps, too, he intends to be more matter-of-fact than one would suppose in the engaging lines:

> Listen! the mighty Being is awake
> And doth with his eternal motion make
> A sound like thunder.

Again, he may be expressing his animism in *Expostulation and Reply*:

> "Nor less I deem that there are Powers
> Which of themselves our minds impress;
> That we can feed this mind of ours
> In a wise passiveness."

These powers, we are led to suppose from passages written for *The Prelude* at about the same time, are no other than the quiet tutelary powers, the powers of earth, that have voices in the clouds and are familiars of the Lakes.

Even more light is thrown upon the puzzling *Peter Bell*. Some readers have had a rather hard time with this poem, because it seems to express the thought that nature exerts a conscious moral influence over men. Since many people are loath to recognize ideas of this kind, they have simply been puzzled and have passed on to other poems. We can now recognize in the work another application of the early animism of Wordsworth. Thus the poet invokes the help of "Dread Spirits" for his wayward Peter:

> Your presence often have I felt
> In darkness and the stormy night;
> And with like force, if need there be,
> Ye can put forth your agency
> When earth is calm, and heaven is bright.

> Then coming from the wayward world,
> That powerful world in which ye dwell,
> Come, Spirits of the Mind! and try,
> To-night, beneath the moonlight sky,
> What may be done with Peter Bell![19]

So the spirits set to work on Peter:

> And now the Spirits of the Mind
> Are busy with poor Peter Bell;
> Upon the rights of visual sense
> Usurping, with a prevalence
> More terrible than magic spell.[20]

Thus was wrought the hallucination which had a large share in Peter's regeneration. The poem was apparently designed to celebrate the power over the mind of the animistic forces that dwell in nature. Probably if the early unrevised text were available, the animism would appear more pronounced and unambiguous.

If anyone feels that this interpretation does violence to a sober-minded poet, he can take comfort in the thought that Wordsworth might be presenting what he conceived to be possible, not what he knew to be true. But the reader should bear in mind that poets commonly have the eccentricity of believing in worlds that their imaginations have fashioned.[21]

V

We have discriminated certain features of Wordsworth's theory of nature: that the external world is free and active; that pleasure resides within outer objects; that value, even outside man, is organic; that form, synthesis, and relation bind external things into close communities; and that Nature exercises a moral influence over man through spirits and tutelary powers that pervade reality. All except the last conviction remained as an element in the poet's most mature thought, and traces of a primitivistic animism may be found even in the later writings. As a final inclusive idea we must consider his pantheism, which bound together these various convictions during the earlier phase of Wordsworth's thought.

Despite his denial of pantheistic convictions in a letter of 1814, we are practically compelled to recognize his early belief that God was at one with man and nature.[22] How else can we interpret "the one interior life":

> —In which all beings live with god, themselves
> Are god, Existing in the mighty whole,
> As indistinguishable as the cloudless East
> At noon is from the cloudless west, when all
> The hemisphere is one cerulean blue.[23]

If any language is pantheistic, this surely is.

Such an outlook came to him at an early age. He definitely records that when his "seventeenth year was come" he had attained the conviction that a unitary "Being" is everywhere:

> . . .in all things now
> I saw one life, and felt that it was joy.[24]

The youth was still fanciful in the application of this new belief; he was too prone to "see blessings spread around" him "like a sea." Yet he had discovered an idea that was to cling to him.

His mature pantheistic view is formulated in *Tintern Abbey* in the lines which are the most perfect expression in English of this philosophy:

> And I have felt
> A presence that disturbs me with the joy
> Of elevated thoughts; a sense sublime
> Of something far more deeply interfused,
> Whose dwelling is the light of setting suns,
> And the round ocean and the living air,
> And the blue sky, and in the mind of man:
> A motion and a spirit, that impels
> All thinking things, all objects of all thought,
> And rolls through all things.

I quote these very familiar verses because I wish to have the exact wording of a disputed passage before the reader. Various protests have been made against calling the lines pantheistic. The passage implies a spirit *dwelling in* things, and therefore distinguished from them. I think what Wordsworth means to suggest is that the spirit must be distinguished from "extension" (Spinoza's term), that is, from mere matter. This distinction was always insisted upon by Spinoza. The proper way to interpret the lines, I think, is to regard them as no more than a partial expression of pantheism; the "presence" is not God, but a part of God. Besides the "motion and the spirit" there is the outer form of the world, or matter; but both spirit and body are ultimately included in the all-embracing unity which is God. Later poems, moreover, suggest an absolute idealism.

A good many passages in the 1805-1806 version of *The Prelude* approach pantheism in tone or suggestion:

> his mind,
> Even as an agent of the one great mind,
> Creates, creator and receiver both.[25]
>
> Thus much for the one Presence, and the Life
> Of the great whole.[26]
>
> Of Genius, Power
> Creation and Divinity itself
> I have been speaking, for my theme has been
> What pass'd within me.[27]

> A soul divine which we participate,
> A deathless spirit.[28]

> . . . God and nature's single sovereignty.[29]

>   . . .a sense,
> Of treachery and desertion in the place
> The holiest that I knew of, my own soul.[30]

>   Great God!
> Who send'st thyself into this breathing world
> Through Nature and through every kind of life,
> And mak'st man what he is, Creature divine.[31]

> The feeling of life endless, the great thought
> By which we live, Infinity and God.[32]

These lines, to a variable extent, state the pantheistic faith that still appeared in traces.

Although by the time *The Prelude* of 1805-1806 was completed, he had abandoned his strict pantheism, he did not entirely eradicate the evidence of his former way of thinking. Yet only in the light of scattered statements and of the indubitable passage concerning "the one interior life," can we construct the proper conception of the early poet. In the 1850 text, he completely removed the evidence of the views he once had held.

For Wordsworth finally deserted his pantheistic position, so that he came to believe in

> . . .God and Man divided, as they ought,
> Between them the great system of the world
> Where Man is sphered, and which God animates.[33]

In another passage he no less clearly withdraws his pantheism. He finds in the timelessness of geometric constructions

> An image not unworthy of the one
> Surpassing Life, which out of space and time,
> Nor touched by welterings of passion, is
> And hath the name of God.[34]

Thus already in the 1805-1806 text of *The Prelude*, Wordsworth expressed a new phase of his philosophy.

But these new ideas did not simply represent a conventional theism. There yet remained a "mighty unity" which embraced all things.[35] The poet still maintained that soul pervades all reality,[36] and that God includes other spirits as the sea her waves.[37]   God was still the "Upholder of the Tranquil Soul" who supplies the mind with forms and measures and principles.[38]   These later convictions fit the scheme of absolute idealism, which conceives of a God, outside of space and time, who yet holds all time and space within his immediate and eternal consciousness.

VI

Apart from these changing points of view, there were certain elements in Wordsworth's philosophy of nature that persisted until the orthodoxy of his late years forced him to abandon the ideas that we think of as Wordsworthian.   What we call "matter," he thought, is the form of things, not the content, and the content eludes the purely analytical thinker.   Mind and nature, since they manifest certain characteristics in common, such as freedom, activity, synthesis, and organic inter-relation, may be considered fundamentally similar in their inner being, although the inorganic world is far more rudimentary than man.   As a consequence of this similarity, the inner order no longer seems so different from the mis-called "mechanical" universe, for underlying all reality is a kind of mindstuff, that in man quickens into a truly magnanimous existence.

of the *Observations on Man,* to which he affixed three essays on the theory of associationism. It was in these that the above statement appears. An influence on Wordsworth is rendered the more probable by his early interest in the republicanism of Priestley and the related group of radicals. There must also have been some contact with Tucker. For several years during the time of Coleridge's closest intimacy with Wordsworth, *The Light of Nature Pursued* was held in high esteem by their circle. So late as 1803 Coleridge still entertained a high opinion of its author.[7] There is every reason to suppose that the same interest that impelled Coleridge and Wordsworth to read Hartley would lead both of them on to a reading of this sequent thinker.

There can be no doubt, at least, that the poet was on the side of the thinkers who recognized most fully the creativeness of the mind.

PROBABLE SOURCES OF WORDSWORTH'S ANIMISM

The animism of Wordsworth must have been stimulated by Coleridge. A number of statements in the latter's poetry indicate the belief in a unitary life that pervades all reality. An interesting example, which resembles some very famous lines in *Tintern Abbey,* occurs in *The Eolian Harp*:

> And what if all of animated nature
> Be but organic Harps diversely fram'd,
> That tremble into thought, as o'er them sweeps
> Plastic and vast, one intellectual breeze,
> At once the Soul of each, and God of all?[1]

Other passages approach closer to Wordsworth's conception of objects in nature that have a certain individuality and yet are organically intertwined:

> Others boldlier think
> That as one body seems the aggregate
> Of atoms numberless, each organized;
> So by a strange and dim similitude
> Infinite myriads of self-conscious minds
> Are one all-conscious Spirit, which informs
> With absolute ubiquity of thought
> (His one eternal self-affirming act!)
> All his involved Monads, that yet seem
> With various province and apt agency
> Each to pursue its own self-centering end.[2]

Another poem indicates that the spirits of nature are interfused and collectively organize matter into appropriate forms:

> Contemplant Spirits! ye that hover o'er
> With untired gaze the immeasureable fount
> Ebullient with creative Deity!
> And ye of plastic power, that interfused
> Roll through the grosser and material mass
> In organizing surge! Holies of God!
> (And what if Monads of the Infinite mind?)[3]

These early passages state animistic doctrines that are not far removed from sentiments expressed by the author of *The Prelude.* Such theories might have furnished support for Wordsworth's idea of life and interaction in the external world.[4]

It is quite likely that Wordsworth learned to know of animistic conceptions from his reading of history and travel. He had a passion for both types of literature. In perusing old travel books he came upon accounts of spirits that dwell in remote regions. He apparently seized upon exactly this source in assisting Coleridge to plot *The Ancient Mariner*:

"Suppose," said I, "you represent him as having killed one of these birds on entering the South Sea, and that the tutelary spirits of these regions take upon them to avenge the crime."[5]

In his report of the time when he first came to believe that there is a life in everything, Wordsworth identifies the conviction with the ideas current in the early cultural stages:

> . . .if things viewed
> By poets in old time, and higher up
> By the first men, earth's first inhabitants,
> May in these tutored days no more be seen
> With undisordered sight.[6]

In *The Excursion*, the poet recounts the mythological ideas of the ancient Persians and Chaldees and Greeks, and indicates his sympathy for their type of nature worship.[7] One suspects that if a similar passage had been introduced into the early text of *The Prelude*, it would have dealt with a period of more primitive thought and would have presented more completely animistic doctrine. At least the first version of *The Prelude* is far more spiritistic than *The Excursion*.

Platonism is another plausible source of the poet's animism. The *Timaeus*, for example, contains an account of God's creation of many spirits to act as his under-agents. Whereupon "the creator sowed some of them in the earth, and some in the moon, and some in the other instruments of time."[8] A good many passages in Plato refer to the conception of demons or geniuses intermediate between God and Man.[9]

This aspect of Plato's thought received a tremendous development among the Neoplatonists. Not only was the world sown far and wide with spirits, but all motion and vegetable growth were accounted for in terms of indwelling spiritual forces.[10] Some such conception of vital presences in vegetation would be almost demanded in order to explain the "faith that every flower enjoys the air it breathes."

It may also be that Wordsworth was influenced by Tucker, whose book he must have read. The author of *The Light of Nature Pursued* conceives of an infinite number of spirits which form collectively a universal soul. All reality is pervaded by this soul and is thus bound together in the closest intercommunication. Every impression made upon a part is immediately transmitted to all the other parts. Thus Wordsworth may have found in Tucker some basis for his conception of a "Soul of all the worlds," or his notion of the solidarity and interpenetration of natural objects.

THE INFLUENCE OF KANT

Among the philosophical influences on Wordsworth, the Kantian is probably one of the most considerable. Yet the evidence is divided and uncertain.

We have two statements of Henry Crabb Robinson, who knew both Germany and Wordsworth, which would tend to show that he regarded the poet's knowledge of German philosophy as quite limited. Although he recorded a "German bent" in Wordsworth's mind,[1] he did not believe that this similarity was based upon firsthand knowledge of the German thinkers. Apropos of a conversation with the poet concerning "imagination," the diarist reports:

> Wordsworth represented, much as unknown to him the German philosophers have done, that by the imagination the mere fact is exhibited in connection with infinity.[2]

In respect to the passage in the *Prospectus* to *The Excursion*, "in which Wordsworth talks of *seeing Jehovah unalarmed*," Robinson also states:

> If Wordsworth means that all notions about the personality of God, as well as the locality of hell, are but attempts to individualize notions concerning Mind, he will be much more of a metaphysical philosopher, *nach deutscher Art*, than I had any conception of.[3]

Clearly Robinson regarded Wordsworth's knowledge of German thought as not very detailed.

The poet himself lends support to the view that the Kantian influence was slight. In a letter of 1840 that he wrote to Robinson, he thus comments upon a "serious charge of Plagiarism brought against Coleridge in the last number of Blackwood":

> With the part concerning the imputation of thefts from Schelling, having never read a word of German metaphysics, thank Heaven! though I doubt not that they are good diet for some tastes, I feel no disposition to meddle.[4]

This declaration is not as conclusive as it appears, for Wordsworth may simply have discovered the vital ideas of the German thinkers through his conversations with Coleridge, rather than through the notoriously cloudy pages of the Teutonic philosophers, who wrote in a language scarcely known to him.

There are some indications of Wordsworth's attachment to Kant and German philosophy. In a sonnet composed in 1809, the author expresses his conviction that the intellectual interests of the world were being jeopardised by Napoleon's subjugation of "sapient Germany":

> Alas! what boots the long laborious quest
> Of moral prudence, sought through good and ill;
> Or pain abstruse—to elevate the will,
> And lead us on to that transcendent rest
> Where every passion shall the sway attest
> Of Reason, seated on her sovereign hill;
> What is it but a vain and curious skill,
> If sapient Germany must lie deprest,
> Beneath the brutal sword?

The poem defines leading elements in two of the principal German philosophical systems: the teaching of both Kant and Fichte sought "to elevate the will"; and Kant endeavored to bring passion under the sway of the Practical Reason, as expressed in the law of duty. The same fear that French aggression would damage German philosophy is expressed in *The Convention of Cintra*.[5] Elsewhere in the tract, when Wordsworth considers the chance of Spanish resistance, he does not mention the philosophers of Spain, but the Spanish literary tradition as constituting the spiritual strength which would generate its own independence. In the case of Germany, on the other hand, he trusts in the solid worth of the inhabitants and the vitality of the philosophy.

A similar high opinion of German thought is conveyed in a letter concerning the Cintra tract, posted March 31, 1809. The poet herein contrasts the degradation of "moral philosophy" in England with "the voice of reason and nature" to be heard in Germany before the French invasion.[6] This statement was made at a time when the utilitarianism of Bentham, Paley, and Adam Smith was regnant in England, and the categorical ethics of Kant and Fichte were in control in Germany. The letter indicates, therefore, Wordsworth's sympathies in one important branch of philosophy.

Another indication of his interest in German speculation is furnished by Thomas G. Gattan, who met Wordsworth and Coleridge in 1828 at Brussels, where he remained with them for three days. He reports that in "all" Wordsworth's "discourse there was a strong flavor of Kantean transcendentalism and mysticism."[7] But

Gattan's testimony may be the result of superficial knowledge, for no person very well informed about Kant would call him mystical.

All the evidence so far cited is overshadowed by the fact of Wordsworth's intimacy with Coleridge, who was tremendously devoted to Kant.[8] How early the latter acquired a knowledge of Kant is difficult to decide, but by 1801, at least, the serious study of the *Critique* commenced.[9] This was in time to affect the first version of *The Prelude* and a large body of additional poetry.

We have a few clues to the elements in the Kantianism of Coleridge that may have impressed Wordsworth. I have previously cited the sonnet in praise of German thought, which *elevated the will* and brought passion under the sway of reason. Now freedom of the will is Kant's supreme postulate of the moral life, and hence Wordsworth was in all probability paying tribute to this aspect of the philosopher's work.

We may partially confirm our suspicion that the poet derived his doctrine of freedom from Kant by comparing two letters written by his friend. On March 16, 1801, Coleridge wrote:

> If I do not greatly delude myself, I have not only *completely extricated the notions of time and space,* but have overthrown the doctrine of associationism, as taught by Hartley, and with it all the irreligious metaphysics of modern infidels—especially the doctrine of necessity.[10]

The words italicized by Coleridge seem surely to indicate a study of Kant; for in the first part of the *Critique of Pure Reason,* the philosopher reveals the ideality of time and space, which are thus extricated from the materialism of the modern infidels. The later argument, moreover, is designed to overthrow the doctrine of necessity, which is central to the entire problem of the work. In a subsequent letter, Coleridge refers again to his "escape from the pernicious doctrine of Necessity," and to the finding of "a better clue than has hitherto been known, to enable others to do the same. I have convinced Southey and Wordsworth. . . ."[11] In view of the fact that Coleridge was much preoccupied with Kant during the lapse of time between the two letters, is it an altogether hazardous inference that the "better clue" was Kant's doctrine of freedom?

I have cited Wordsworth's commendation of the moral philosophy of Germany. This praise leads us to expect that his theory of duty and the moral life was influenced by German thought. The poem that is usually cited as evidence is the *Ode to Duty.* The identification is made more likely by the character of the third stanza, which seems to be based upon Schiller's idea of the "beautiful soul," a conception advanced in controversy with Kant. On the other hand, we know that Wordsworth read Vaughan, and in two of the poems of Vaughan we find ideas that might explain the apparent echoing of Kant and Schiller. In *Misery* occurs the contrast between being to oneself a guide and being the happy bondsman of God. In *The Constellation* appears the declaration that the same laws that are exemplified by "Thy whole creation," and by the stars in particular, should be binding upon the individual human heart.[12] Kant similarly compared the austere sublimity of the stars with the categorical imperative. Also he maintained, like Vaughan and Wordsworth, that duty is the "Stern Daughter of the Voice of God" and is binding upon all thinking creatures and even upon the Infinite Being.[13] In the face of this agreement, I can see no way to decide just what influence is to be traced in the *Ode*. It is altogether possible, of course, that the author was indebted to both sources.

Kant maintained that another way of formulating his conception of duty is in his concept of a Kingdom of Ends. This doctrine, that every being should be treated as an end, never as a means, is precisely summarized in a passage of *The Excursion*:

> Our life is turned
> Out of her course, wherever man is made
> An offering, or a sacrifice, a tool
> Or implement, a passive thing employed
> As a brute mean, without acknowledgment
> Of common right or interest in the end;
> Used or abused, as selfishness may prompt.
> Say, what can follow for a rational soul
> Perverted thus, but weakness in all good,
> And strength in evil?[14]

Thus Wordsworth appears to have accepted the two main principles of the Kantian ethics: the categorical imperative and the doctrine of ends.

I have discussed in chapter IV Kant's criticism of associationism and his alternative theory of the transcendental imagination. This section of the *Critique* unquestionably impressed Coleridge, and doubtless was made known to Wordsworth. Kant's transcendentalism also involved a distinction between the discursive and originative faculties of the mind. The lower reason merely treads helplessly within the same round of an experience imposed and non-extensible; whereas the higher reason leaps clear of experience to an inward determination of the conditions of life and thought.[15] Wordsworth implies this distinction in the two passages from *The Prelude* in which he most expressly states his obligation to Coleridge.[16] In the first passage, he contrasts the "false secondary power by which we multiply distinctions" with the "words of Reason deeply weighed." In the second, he speaks of "a Reason which indeed is reason." These two statements, occurring where they do, make it appear very likely that the discrimination between the higher and lower reason was derived from Kant through the mediation of Coleridge.

Wordsworth may also have been impressed by the Kantian theory of the "unity of apperception," which points to a unification of reality both within and beyond experience. He may be obliquely referring in some degree to this conception when he says of Coleridge:

> To thee, unblinded by these formal arts,
> The unity of all hath been revealed.[17]

Kant also maintained, like Wordsworth, that the mind and the senses work together in the very closest interdependence. The best known statement of this position is the famous dictum: "Thoughts without content are empty; intuitions without concepts are blind." In the section of the *Critique* called "The Transcendental Deduction of the Categories," Kant takes the position that the mind can only come to know itself by contrast with the outer world.

This summary indicates that there are grounds for inferring an important Kantian influence on Wordsworth.

NOTES

CHAPTER I

[1] Wordsworth's *Prose Works,* ed. Grosart, III, p. 469.
The references are listed complete in my final bibliography.

[2] "Every poet is a teacher," he said; "I wish either to be considered as a teacher or as nothing." (*Memorials of Coleorton,* ed. by William Knight, II, 31). Elsewhere in his correspondence he asserted: "There is scarcely any one of my poems which does not aim to direct the attention to some moral sentiment, or to some general principle, or law of thought, or of our intellectual constitution." (*Ibid.,* II, 12). See also Henry Crabb Robinson, *Diary, Reminiscenses and Correspondence,* I. p. 266; and *Prelude* (1850 text), I, 227-233.

[3] *Prelude,* VI, 241-247, All references to *The Prelude* are to the 1850 version unless otherwise stated. Significant variants in the earlier text will be noted. Whenever the 1850 reading represents an entirely new addition, that also will be indicated. The De Selincourt text is followed throughout.

[4] See *Prelude,* 1805-1806 text, X, 905-908.

[5] *Ibid.,* VI, 263.

[6] See *Letters of Wordsworth Family,* III, p. 462; and *Memorials of Coleorton,* I, p. 101.

[7] *Herrig's Archiv fur das studium der neureren sprachen und litteraturen,* XCVII (1896), p. 354. Lamb had learned of this intention by June, 1796. Lamb, *Works,* VI, p. 27.

[8] *Letters,* I, pp. 348-349.

[9] *Ibid.,* II, p. 454.

[10] *Excursion,* IX, 1-19; and the sonnet, "A Poet!—He hath put his heart to school."

[11] *Letters,* p. 16.

[12] For example, he shunned the division of perceptions into small space and time units: *Anima Poetae,* pp. 102-103; passage written in 1804.

[13] Cottle, *Early Recollections,* II, p. 234; note affixed to Southey's *Joan of Arc.*

[14] *Letters,* I, pp. 348-349.

[15] *Ibid.,* p. 428.

[16] Since Coleridge has been represented as exercising a predominantly Hartleian influence on Wordsworth, I list further evidence: *Biographia Literaria,* I, p. 98, which indicates the influence of the mystics on Coleridge during his most Hartleian period; *ibid.,* p. 93, which records a dissatisfaction with Locke, Berkeley, and Hartley prior to the serious study of Kant and before any real familiarity with Behmen (for evidence of early reading of Behmen see *Archiv, op. cit.,* pp. 333-372); Cottle, *op. cit.,* pp. 21-22, which testifies that Coleridge's enthusiasm for Hartley during 1795 soon gave way; *Archiv, ibid.,* which contains scattered revelations of an un-Hartleian state of mind from 1796 to the spring or summer of 1798; Coleridge's Poems, 1797 edition, note to the poem "To a Friend," a rejection of Hartley's necessitarianism; Coleridge's comment on *The Destiny of Nations,* quoted by S. F. Gingerich, *Proceedings of the Modern Language Association,* XXXV (1920), p. 23; Clement Carlyon, *Early Years and Late Reflections,* I, pp. 33-34, 90, 92-93, 119, 193, 195 f.n., passages which prove that Coleridge in 1799 was very much attracted by Bruno and Spinoza, who are very widely separated from Hartley, and that his liking for associationism did not prevent attachment to quite opposing views; Hazlitt, *My First Acquaintance with Poets,* second paragraph from end, in which the Coleridge of 1798 agrees with

Hazlitt that the "association of ideas" is inadequate to explain our recognitions of resemblance (in Hartley's system, similarity is due to identity in content, a view which Hazlitt and Coleridge reject); A. Turnbull, *Biographia Epistolaris,* I, p. 274 and *ante,* a letter of June 4, 1863, in which Coleridge speaks of an intention of writing a summary of Hartley, but also reveals a great interest in Plato and Kant, who are at the opposite pole from Hartley; *ibid.,* I, p. 224, which indicates an abandonment of associationistic ideas early in 1801; Coleridge, *Letters,* I, p. 358, in which the writer declares in July, 1801, that "Locke, Hume, and Hobbes   . . . stink worse than feather or assafoetida"; De Quincey, *Works* (ed. Adam and Charles Black), II, p. 56, in which the author states that Coleridge's devotion to Hartley was "a forgotten thing" by August, 1807; *Anima Poetae,* pp. 151-152, which announces his mature philosophical allegiances. Compare Arthur Beatty, *William Wordsworth: His Doctrine and Art in Their Historical Relations,* pp. 100-102. Professor Beatty's comment upon Hazlitt's essay is especially misleading: "Hazlitt's account of his visit to the joint authors of the *Lyrical Ballads.* . .shows that benevolence and association, two fundamentals in the system of Hartley, were fully accepted by Coleridge." A careful reading of the essay will reveal that "the theory of disinterestedness" (benevolence) was Hazlitt's, not Coleridge's, and was derived from Bishop Butler, an opponent of Hartley. It will also disclose that the mention of "association of ideas" emanated from Hazlitt, and that Coleridge merely agreed to its inadequacy. This evidence is in harmony with the conclusions of John H. Muirhead, *Coleridge as a Philosopher,* pp. 40-46.

    [17] *Prelude,* II, 206-232; 1805-1806 version almost identical.

    [18] The view that the content of consciousness derives not solely from experience, but to some extent from the mind's internal stores. The orthodox conception of conscience is a familiar illustration.

    [19] *Herrig's Archiv, op. cit.*

    [20] *Biographia Literaria,* I, p. 94.

    [21] *Memorials of Coleorton,* I, p. 64. Letter of December 17, 1808.

    [22] *Aids to Reflection,* under aphorism viii.

    [23] *Works,* ed. Shedd, II, p. 286.

    [24] *Prelude,* VIII, 671-672.

    [25] In the quotation reproduced below.

    [26] See *Anima Poetae,* pp. 35-36.

    [27] *Prelude* (1805-1806), XIII, 246-268.

    [28] See *Letters,* p. 353.

    [29] *Anima Poetae,* pp. 180, 128-129.

    [30] *Ibid.,* p. 15; also Walter Graham, *An Important Coleridge Letter, Journal of English and Germanic Philology,* XXI, pp. 530-535; and *Biographia Epistolaris,* I, p. 261.

    [31] *Anima Poetae,* p. 77.

CHAPTER II

    [1] "Convention of Cintra," *Prose Works,* I, p. 171.

    [2] *Prelude* (1805-1806), II, 237-280; (1850), 233-265.

    [3] Letter of Professor Bonamy Price, quoted by William Knight, *Poetical Works of William Wordsworth,* pp. 201-202; see also Fenwick, note to *Ode: Intimations of Immortality,* and Grosart, *Prose Works,* III, p. 467.

    [4] The reader will recognize a Platonic flavoring to this interpretation of the *Ode.* It should be noted that all influences on the poem that have been so far proved have been Platonic. Wordsworth himself mentions Plato in connection with the poem in his Fenwick note, and Coleridge also brings up Plato when he discusses the *Ode* in the *Biographia Literaria.* John D. Rea has practically demonstrated the influence of Proclus on sections v-viii of

the poem ("Coleridge's Intimations of Immortality from Proclus," *Modern Philology*, November, 1928, pp. 201-213; a very important article). The probable influence of Henry Vaughan, a poet saturated with neo-Platonism, has been established by Grosart (*Henry Vaughan's Works, Fuller Worthies Library*, II, pp. lxii-lxviii) and by L. R. Merill ("Vaughan's Influence upon Wordsworth's Poetry, *Modern Language Notes*, February, 1922, pp. 91-96). Frederick E. Pierce has argued persuasively that Wordsworth may be indebted in the poem to Thomas Taylor's *Works of Plato* and that a comparison reveals many parallels ("Wordsworth and Thomas Taylor," *Philological Quarterly*, January, 1928, pp. 60-64).

⁵ *Prelude*, I, 391-392.

⁶ *Composed Upon an Evening of Extraordinary Splendour and Beauty,* IV.

⁷ Wordsworth may be following Rousseau in the view that the stage of reason arrives late, and is preceded by the stage of emotion. (See *Emile*, Everyman's Library, pp. 131, 134, 165, 220). Also the Rousselian doctrine that abstract ideas are quite beyond the child is admirably illustrated in *We Are Seven* and *An Anecdote for Fathers*.

⁸ V, 552-556. But the 1805-1806 version substitutes "thirteen years."

⁹ V, 577-583.

¹⁰ I, 562-566.

¹¹ *Prelude*, II, 358-374.

¹² *Cf.* Beatty, *op. cit.*, p. 80.

¹³ *Prelude*, II, 386-392.

¹⁴ *Ibid.*, XIV, 345-347.

¹⁵ *Ibid.*, VIII, 376-420.

¹⁶ *Ibid.*, III, 130-135.

¹⁷ *Ibid.*, III, 149-196.

¹⁸ *Ibid.*, IV, 307-338.

¹⁹ *Ibid.*, IV, 150-152; next quotation follows.

²⁰ *Ibid.* (1805-1806), VIII, 630-633. The rest of the passage is interesting for its pantheistic and transcendental drift.

²¹ *Ibid.* (1805-1806), III, variant reading for lines 207-210.

²² This paragraph is based upon Book III.

²³ *Ibid.*, later text VI, 624-640.

²⁴ *Cf.* De Selincourt, p. 562. When Wordsworth says in V, 552-553 that "not less than two and twenty summers had been told" when he attained to this stage, he must mean that he had reached twenty-two, not that he had completed his twenty-second year. No other chronology would agree with the objective facts.

²⁵ *Prelude* (1805-1806), XI, 74-88.

²⁶ *Ibid.*, 121-137.

²⁷ *Ibid.*, later text, XII, 114-115, 140-147.

²⁸ *Ibid.*, XII, 126.

²⁹ See the note of De Selincourt, *op. cit.*, pp. 584-587, 592. *The Prelude*, XII, 109-131, has been misinterpreted. Professor Beatty has taken the last four lines as characterizing childhood and youth, not as pertaining to early manhood (*cf., op. cit.*, p. 88). He has been led astray by the word "recollection," which suggests return in memory to an earlier phase of consciousness. But what Wordsworth means is that he recollects, while writing at a later time, a state of mind which he had experienced in early manhood. The earlier text makes the true meaning indubitable:

> The state to which I now allude was one
> In which the eye was master of the heart,
> When that which is in every stage of life
> The most despotic of our senses gain'd, etc.

These lines, read in the context supplied for them, can have only one meaning.

³⁰ Many scholars, including Legouis, Harper, and Babbitt, have found

evidence in Wordsworth's attitude toward reason that he was devoted to Rousseau. The contention is plausible, for the resemblances between the two writers are striking and the poet's knowledge of Rousseau is incontestable. Much more debatable is his mature acceptance of Rousselian theories, for a decided anti-French bias, which extends to all books and thinkers, appears in a sonnet, "Great men have been among us," probably written in September, 1802, but at least as early as 1803. One might answer that the poem expresses a temporary extreme of reaction which time must have rectified. Yet in *The Convention of Cintra,* written in 1807, Wordsworth reaffirms his opposition to French thought and includes a derogatory reference to the author of *Emile* (*Prose Works,* I, pp. 161-162). In the face of these declarations, it is impossible to maintain that Wordsworth's main dependence as a thinker was upon Rousseau. The explanation of the resemblances between the two writers may perhaps be found in the convergence of Rousseau's views with those of other speculators. To a remarkable degree he reformulated ideas that had already been expressed or were then in the air. We are thus prevented from using the comparative method as a test for detecting influence. A summary of the correspondences between Rousseau and Shaftesbury will help to make the difficulty clear. They share fundamental tenets: that one should venerate "nature" in nearly all the senses of the word; that Hobbes' account of the "state of nature" and the rise of the social contract is false; that the orginal part of man's mental constitution is good, and that accordingly conscience is an original affection of earliest rise in the soul; that the merely intellectual processes of the mind are suspect, and that hence there must be a large cultivation of the senses and the feelings; that constructive Deism is correct in its major contention that God may be logically inferred from nature. In consequence, Wordsworth does not solely resemble Rousseau, but shows a marked resemblance to Shaftesbury. In certain respects, he is nearer to the English thinker. He is in closer accord with Shaftesbury's tendency to regard God as the soul of nature than with Rousseau's relatively sharp distinction between God and His creation. He shares with Shaftesbury an idea not developed in Rousseau, that the aesthetic faculties are very important instruments in the search for truth. These similarities loom as significant in view of Wordsworth's appreciative reference to Shaftesbury in the *Essay, Supplementary to the Preface,* and in view of the fact that an early edition of Shaftesbury was in his library. The facts in general seem to be that Rousseau early exercised a considerable sway over the poet but that this influence had greatly abated by September, 1802. The poet nevertheless retained the Rousselian conviction of man's innate goodness and of the need to "draw out" human nature (see *Prose Works,* I, p. 343). Moreover a comparison of their interpretation of the development of personality will reveal similarity if not derivation: since the higher states are thought to rest upon the lower, which must be developed first in point of time.

[31] The remainder of the line is illegible in the present state of the manuscript.

[32] Pp. 512-513. *Cf.* II, 216-219, quoted above, beginning "Of that false secondary power etc." The 1805 version reproduces the wording of the four lines without change.

[33] II, 220-221.

[34] *Ibid.* (1805-1806) XIII, 267-268.

[35] At the Cleveland meeting of the Modern Language Association, 1929-1930, a prominent Wordsworthian scholar spoke with some little scorn of the people who foster the "myth" that Wordsworth was affected by mysticism.

[36] Lines 637-690. Cr. the comment on this passage by Barry Cerf, "Wordsworth's Gospel of Nature," *Publications of Mod. Lang. Assn.,* XXXVII (1922), pp. 615-638.

[37] *The Sparrow's Nest.*

[38] *Cf., Paradise Lost,* V. 404-418, 469-488. The last part of the passage from Milton is quoted by Coleridge in the *Biographia Literaria,* and the last

line seems to be echoed by Wordsworth, *Prelude,* XIV, 120, in close proximity to another Miltonic phrase (*cf.* De Selincourt, p. 605). Also the phrase, "bright consummate flower," is quoted by Wordsworth in "The Convention of Cintra," *Prose Works,* I, p. 171. Wordsworth thus appears to be partially indebted to Milton for the most basic of all his moral conceptions.

³⁹ XII, 277-284. 1805-1806 version substantially the same.

⁴⁰ Lines 65-80.

CHAPTER III

¹ Reproduced from mss. in the British Museum by Alice D. Snyder, *Coleridge on Logic and Learning,* p. 119.

² *Statesman,* 278, Jowett's translation. The numbering refers to the standard divisions in the text.

³ *Symposium,* 211.

⁴ *Antidote Against Atheism,* bk. I, ch. V, sec. 2. Coleridge had a great admiration for Henry More, and very likely conveyed to Wordsworth something of his appreciation.

⁵ *Prelude,* VI, 604-605.

⁶ *Ibid.,* V, 507-511.

⁷ *Ibid.* (1805-1806), VI, 150-156. *Cf.* 1850 version, 129-141. Note that pantheism has been formally renounced even in the 1805-1806 text.

⁸ We have strong supplementary evidence of Platonic influence. Coleridge's two great philosophical passions were German metaphysics and Platonism, and there can be no question that he presented to Wordsworth many Platonic conceptions. The books in the poet's library would seem to indicate a decided interest in Plato. The volumes in the Platonic tradition include Paracelsus, Jacob Behmen, Edward Taylor's exposition of Behmen's theosophy, Clement of Alexandria, Richard Cudworth, Thomas Taylor's annotated edition of the *Cratylus, Phaedo, Parmenides,* and *Timaeus* (ed. of 1793), Schleiermacher's *Introduction to the Dialogues of Plato* (1836), and *Platonis Dialogi* V (1752). Five references to Plato (more than to any other thinker) occur in the complete poetical works, exclusive of the manuscripts of the early *Prelude.* One of the manuscripts contains a very complimentary reference to Plato (De Selincourt, p. 590). In *The Convention of Cintra,* Wordsworth declares that in the persons of Plato, Demosthenes, Homer, Shakespeare, Milton, and Lord Bacon "were enshrined as much of the divinity of intellect as the inhabitants of this planet can hope will ever take up its abode among them" (*Prose Works,* I, p. 312). The poet in conversation once remarked that Plato's *Phaedo,* Shakespeare's *Othello,* and Walton's *Life of George Herbert* were "the most pathetic of human compositions" (Christopher Wordsworth, *Memoirs of William Wordsworth,* II, p. 482). The similarities between Plato and Wordsworth are impressive. The poet defines God in the Platonic mode as rational or ideal: "Thou Soul that art the eternity of thought" (*Prelude,* I, 402). Like the Platonists, he conceived of a soul of the World that includes all material entities (*Excursion,* IX, 1-15; *cf. Timaeus,* 30-31, and Henry More, *The Immortality of the Soul,* III, xii, sec. 1). He accepted what is probably the most fundamental of all the Platonic doctrines, the conception of "forms" (see "Brook! whose society the Poet seeks," and Sonnet XXXIV of *The River Duddon*). Wordsworth agrees with Platonism in his conception of the co-working of the senses and the transcendental powers of the mind. It was no doubt a personal tendency, but none the less in accord with Platonism, to commune through sense with what lies beyond sense, to look on nature, and "see into the life of things." He is also in accord with Plato in his intimations of immortality. Not only did he make use in the *Ode* of the Platonic "recol-

lection" of pre-existence, but the entire poem follows the *Phaedo* in emphasiz-
ing the "high instincts" by which our "mortal Nature" appears a pensioner
upon the immortal elements of the mind. To find a similar glorification of
childhood we cannot do better than to read the Platonists—Proclus, Hermes
Trismegistus, Henry Vaughan, Thomas Traherne, Thomas Taylor, and even
Plato himself in the *Phaedrus*. In Appendix B, I point out the possible connection between Platonism and Wordsworth's animism.

[9] See John D. Rea, *op. cit.,* pp. 201, 209-211.

[10] See the Fenwick note which prefaces the *Ode* in most editions.

[11] *Biographia Literaria,* (ed. Shawcross), II, pp. 120-121. Italics are mine.

[12] "Those Words Were Uttered as in Pensive Mood."

[13] To quote all the other strong evidence of his transcendentalism would
overcrowd these pages; but at least I can indicate where much of it may be
found: *Recluse,* 763-766 and 772-775; *Prelude,* VI, 166-168; 1805-1806 text
of *Prelude,* III, 109-120, and VIII, 637-639, and XIII, 101-106; *Excursion,*
IV, 50-56 and 1126-1132. A good deal of additional evidence from Wordsworth's works is cited in the latter part of this chapter.

[14] "The mind is lord and master—outward sense
The obedient servant of her will."—*Prelude,* XII, 222-223.

[15] I quote from the early ms. version in the possession of Gordon Wordsworth and reproduced in the variant readings of Ernest Hartley Coleridge's
edition of the poems. The remainder of the poem is interesting. It contains, for example, the phrase, "chosen Laws controlling choice," which contrasts with the necessitarianism of Godwin and Hartley.

[16] *Letters,* II, pp. 641-642.

[17] *Ibid.,* p. 648. Note the similarity of wording between this passage
and the one from Coleridge's *Table Talk* quoted in the present chapter. He
is evidently recalling the plan which the two poets had worked out during
the early stages of their association.

[18] 1805-1806 version, 70-72.

[19] See *Prelude* (1805-1806), XIII, 149-165.

[20] *Ibid.,* V, 16.

[21] *Ibid.,* XIII, 107-111. *Cf.* the following apostrophe to God from *The
Excursion*:

> thou, thou alone
> Art everlasting, and the blessed Spirits,
> Which thou includest, like the sea her waves.   (IV, 91-93).

[22] *Prose Works,* I, pp. 153-154.

[23] *Prelude* (1805-1806) VIII, 823-835. It does not contradict transcendentalism to assert as Wordsworth does in the *Letter to "Mathetes"*: "Our
eyes have not been fixed upon virtue which lies apart from human nature,
or transcends it. In fact, there is no such virtue." Kant also maintained
that the categorical imperative, although binding upon every spirit including God, can be discovered by the simplest laborer. Wordsworth's conception of human nature, in addition, was so august that almost nothing seemed
beyond it.

[24] *Cf. The Excursion,* IV, 94-99:

> . . .endure
> For consciousness the motions of thy will;
> For apprehension those transcendent truths;
> Of the pure intellect, that stand as laws. . .
> Even to thy Being's infinite majesty!

[25] See *ibid.,* 73-76.

[26] *Ibid.,* 222-227.

[27] *Prelude,* III, 83-85. Not in 1805-1806 text.

[28] *Ibid.* (1805-1806), X, 386-393.

[29] *Ibid.* (1805-1806), XIII, 164-188.

[30] *Ibid.* (1850), VI, 592-605.

[31] This interpretation may be buttressed by Thomas De Quincey's well

known essay, *Literature of Knowledge and Literature of Power.* This composition first appeared in the *North British Review* for August, 1848. But 25 years earlier De Quincey had set forth the same distinction in his *Letters to a Young Man.* He definitely attributed the thought of the essay to Wordsworth:

> "For which the above distinction, as for most sound criticism on poetry, or any subject connected with it that I have ever met with, I must acknowledge my obligations to many years conversation with Mr. Wordsworth." (*Works,* ed. Masson, X, p. 48).

It is therefore significant in our present study to find the literature of power, the literature, that is, of genuine imagination, dealt with in transcendental terms; it is the product of "the great *intuitive* (or non-discursive) organ," which is "the interchangeable formula for man in his highest state of capacity for the infinite." But see the entire essay.

[32] *Ibid.* (1805-1806) XII, 373-374. See the accompanying lines from which the next quoted phrase is taken.

[33] Probably Wordsworth would have tempered his language if the poem had been written later, for he grew less naturistic and more conservative. Even if we should decide that the passage in *Tintern Abbey* excludes transcendentalism, we have no reason to suppose that later transcendentalistic utterances are not to be trusted. The poet changed his mind in other respects; why not in this? But there seems to be no reason why we should not accept the explanation of the text proffered above. We must remember that it was near the time of the poem's composition that Wordsworth penned the highly mystical passage in which he says that "one interior life. . .lives in all things," that "all beings live with god, themselves are god."

[34] Fragment from Ms. Y, reproduced by De Selincourt, *op. cit.,* p. 557.

CHAPTER IV

[1] *Song at the Feast of Brougham Castle,* 161-164.

[2] The direct evidence of Wordsworth's indebtedness to Hartley is slight. See my article, "The Transcendentalism of William Wordsworth," *Modern Philology,* November, 1928. The only telling evidence is contained in the *Preface* to the *Lyrical Ballads* in which the author states that his purpose was "above all" to make "the incidents and situations" of common life "interesting by tracing in them, truly though not ostentatiously, the primary laws of our nature: chiefly, as far as regards the manner in which we associate ideas in a state of excitement." *The Preface,* both in the 1800 version and the 1802 revision, contains other associationistic language. We must remember in this connection that the *Lyrical Ballads* are probably more associationistic than any later publication of Wordsworth. Professor Beatty, *op. cit.,* pp. 97-102, has misread and misinterpreted some of the other evidence of Hartleian influence. For the necessary corrections see my article on Wordsworth's transcendentalism and my discussion of Coleridge's relation to Hartley in chapter I. Despite Mr. Beatty's over-emphasis he has performed a large service to English criticism in firmly establishing the fact that the poet employs the language of associationism in a good many passages.

[3] Hartley's language is as follows:

"Sensations may be said to be associated together, when their impressions are either made precisely at the same Instant of Time, or in contiguous successive instants." (*Observations on Man,* I, prop. x.)

"Sensations, by being often repeated, leave certain vestiges, types, or images, of themselves, which may be called, Simple Ideas of Sensation." (*Ibid.,* prop. viii.)

"Any sensations, A, B, C, etc., by being associated with one another a sufficient number of times, get such a power over the corresponding ideas, a, b, c, etc., that any one of the sensations A, when impressed alone, shall be able to excite in the mind b, c, etc., the ideas of the rest." (Prop. x.)

"And upon the whole, it may appear to the reader, that the simple ideas of sensation must run into clusters and combinations by association, and these will at last coalesce into one complex idea, by the approach and commixture of the several compounding parts." (Prop. xii.)

[4] *Prelude*, I, 407-409.

[5] James Gibson, *Locke's Theory of Knowledge*, pp. 47-48. The book gives an excellent exposition of the point of view from which Wordsworth took his departure.

[6] In appendix A, I trace the development of the modern view among those thinkers whom Wordsworth must have read.

[7] *Poems on the Naming of Places*, I. Compare the comment of E. H. Sneath, *Wordsworth: Poet of Nature and Poet of Man*, p. 159.

[8] *Science and the Modern World*, pp. 121-122. By "prehension" Mr. Whitehead means unconscious apprehension, somewhat after the fashion of the mirroring of the world by Leibnitz's monads, but without the pluralism of the Leibnitzian system.

[9] I, 464-475.

[10] This aspect of Wordsworth's thought is seized upon by Whitehead, *op. cit.*, pp. 120-122.

[11] 1805-1806 text, 29-65. The corresponding lines in the 1850 version, like so many passages in the revision, polish the language but obscure the thought.

[12] *Ibid.*, 73-84.

[13] Contiguity may be of two kinds, simultaneity or succession; i.e., occurrence at the same instant of time, or in contiguous successive instants. See Hartley, *op. cit.*, prop. x.

[14] *Critique of Pure Reason*, pp. 84-85.

[15] For Kant's complete statement, see Norman Kemp Smith, *Commentary to Kant's Critique of Pure Reason*, p. 266. These ideas of Kant are developed at length, so that Coleridge could not have missed them.

[16] *Ibid.*

[17] In appendix C, I review the further evidence of Kant's influence.

[18] An instructive application is to be found in *Prelude*, XII, 208-335. The passage is too long to quote.

[19] See Hazlitt's testimony in *The Spirit of the Age*, 1825, and traces of necessitarianism in *The Borderers*. The murderer in *Guilt and Sorrow* seems to have been a victim of necessity.

[20] "Philosophical Necessity," Hazlitt's *Works*, XI, 277-278.

[21] Lines 286-288.

[22] Lines 296-297. Cf. the poem *Ruth*, in which the hero's development is obstructed by "irregularity" and "impetuosity." Also compare *The Excursion*, with its portrait of the Solitary, upon whom nature had an evil effect because he lacked a spiritual and imaginative approach.

[23] It is instructive to contrast this position with the full-fledged necessitarianism of Hartley. He supposes that mental growth is so certain and rigid that the process, if indefinitely extended under the same environmental influences would reduce everybody to the identity of indiscernibles! He says: "If beings of the same nature, but whose affections and passions are, at present, in different proportions to each other, be exposed for an indefinite time to the same impressions and associations, all their particular differences, will, at last, be overruled, and they will become perfectly similar, or even equal. They may also be made perfectly similar in a finite time, by a proper adjustment of the impressions and associations." (*Op. cit.*, prop. xiv, cor. 6.) If by manipulation of stimuli, men might be reduced in a finite time to perfectly similar creatures, even equals, then the inward factors must be of no avail except insofar as they are strictly derivative from the outside. It is clear that this view makes man a machine. Although pleasure and pain, in

Hartley's psychology, contribute to the strength and celerity of associational processes, even these emotions are derivative in the first instance from sensation and association (see p. 513, *ibid.*, edition of 1810).

CHAPTER V

[1] From Lamb's review of *The Excursion, Quarterly Review,* October, 1814. Reproduced by Alfred Ainger, "Wordsworth and Charles Lamb," *Wordsworthiana,* pp. 246-247.

[2] "A Poet!—He Hath Put His Heart to School."

[3] IX, 1-18.

[4] II, 266.

[5] XI (1805-1806), 139, 146-147. Only line 139 is reproduced in the corresponding 1850 text, XII, 94.

[6] *The Kitten and Falling Leaves,* 95-103.

[7] As in Lord Morley's introduction to *The Complete Poetical Works of William Wordsworth,* p. lxv.

[8] *The Old Cumberland Beggar,* 11, 77-79.

[9] *Ode,* "Imagination—ne'er before content," 106-109, version of 1816.

[10] Lines 73-179.

[11] *Excursion,* IX, 10-14.

[12] For example, see *Excursion,* IV, 957-966.

[13] "The Sylvan Slopes with Corn-Clad Fields."

[14] VIII, corresponding to lines 55-69 in the 1850 version and lines 46-61 in the 1805-1806 text. The variant reading begins at line 55 of the 1805-1806 version.

[15] Corresponding to 351-375 in the 1805-1806 text, and 340-361 in the 1850 reading. The version of 1805-1806 still retains a strong flavor of the original.

[16] V, 491-495. Same in 1805-1806.

[17] Variant reading for I, 490-492 in 1805-1806 text.

[18] Lines 165-168.

[19] Lines 776-785. It is clear from these stanzas that the spirits dwell in nature, even though they are called "Spirits of the Mind."

[20] 916-920.

[21] In appendix B, I trace the probable sources of Wordsworth's animism.

[22] Knight, *Letters of the Wordsworth Family,* II, pp. 41-43. The letter not only denies the identification of nature and God, but repudiates the charge that the poet's thought is Spinozistic. It must be remembered, however, that the letter was written subsequent to the publication of *The Excursion* in 1814, and it is therefore no accurate index of the writer's earlier convictions. The latter part of the letter, moreover, proves that his position corresponded with Spinoza in an important respect: the philosopher also inveighed against the idea of "making by God," and sought to prove that "God is the indwelling and not the transient cause of all things" (*Ethic,* pt. I, prop. xviii). It is well known that Coleridge was devoted to the Jewish thinker during the early years of his intimacy with Wordsworth. He records their discussion of Spinoza (*Biographia Literaria,* I, p. 127). It is important to know what aspects of Spinoza Wordsworth would have thus learned about from Coleridge. Carlyon, who became acquainted with the latter in Germany, supplies the clue; he declares that Coleridge's concentrated definition of Spinozism was, "Each thing has a life of its own, and we are all one life." (*Op. cit.* p. 193). This definition embraces two aspects of Spinoza's thought. First, we have his doctrine of psycho-physical parallelism: of the infinite attributes of God, man grasps but two, thought and extension; God or nature always has these two aspects, body and mind. One can not occur without the other,

because both are essential to the nature of substance. Second, we find in Spinoza a monistic pantheism; God is not an external contriver, but an immanent, all-pervading, and indivisible presence; Nature and God are one. These ideas are reflected in Wordsworth, whether he derived them from Spinoza or not.

[23] De Selincourt, *op. cit.*, pp. 512-513.

[24] *Prelude* (1805-1806), II, 429-430. Compare *Excursion*, I, 148-162. wherein the idealistic implications are very explicit.

[25] II, 271-273.

[26] III, 130-131.

[27] III, 171-174.

[28] V, 16-17.

[29] IX, 237.

[30] IX, 379-381.

[31] X, 386-389.

[32] XIII, 183-184.

[33] XIII, 266-268.

[34] VI, 154-157.

[35] *Prelude* (1805-1806), XIII, 254-255; (1850), VI, 636-640, same in 1805-1806 text.

[36] *Excursion*, beginning of IX.

[37] *Ibid.*, IV, 91-93.

[38] *Ibid.*, IV, 28, 73-76.

APPENDIX A

[1] *Essay Concerning Human Understanding*, bk. III, ch. iii, sec. 2.

[2] *Cf.* James Gibson, *Locke's Theory of Knowledge*, pp. 63-70, 115-119.

[3] *Observations on Man*, I, pp. 370-371.

[4] *Ibid.*, prop. xi.

[5] *The Light of Nature Pursued*, ch. XII, art. 1. The statement occurs in a chapter on "Imagination and Understanding," a title which would unquestionably interest Wordsworth.

[6] Essay III, *Miscellaneous Works*, ed. of 1818, III, p. 190.

[7] See *Biographia Epistolaris*, I, p. 274.

APPENDIX B

[1] Lines 44-48. Written August 20, 1795.

[2] *The Destiny of Nations*, 39-49. Poem completed in 1796.

[3] *Religious Musings*, 402-408. Written 1794-1796.

[4] See J. H. Muirhead, *op. cit.*, pp. 121-130, for later evidence of Coleridge's spiritualistic interpretation of nature. *Dejection: An Ode*, the first version of which was written April 4, 1802, appears to represent a temporary abandonment of idealism: "And in *our* life alone does Nature live!"

[5] The author's note to "We Are Seven."

[6] *Prelude*, III, 153-157. Same in 1805-1806 text.

[7] IV, 663-762.

[8] Jowett, 42.

[9] See Jowett's index, vol. V, p. 400.

[10] See, for example, Henry More, *The Immortality of the Soul*, bk. 1, ch. VIII, sec. 3.

APPENDIX C

[1] *Diary,* I, p. 482.

[2] *Ibid.,* II, p. 24. September 11, 1816.

[3] *Ibid.,* I, p. 465. December 18, 1814.

[4] *The Correspondence of Henry Crabb Robinson with the Wordsworth Circle,* p. 401.

[5] *Prose Works,* I, pp. 171-172.

[6] *Letters From the Lake Poets to Daniel Stuart,* pp. 334-335.

[7] *Beaten Paths,* II, pp. 107f. Quoted by Max J. Herzberg, "William Wordsworth and German Literature," *P.M.L.A.,* vol. XL, p. 324.

[8] ". . .I reverence Immanuel Kant with my whole heart and soul, and believe him to be the only philosopher, for *all men* who have the power of thinking. I cannot conceive the liberal pursuit or profession, in which the service derived from a patient study of his works would not be incalculably great. . . ." *Letters,* II, p. 682; written in 1817.

[9] See F. W. Stokoe, *German Influence in the English Romantic Period,* especially pp. 90-91 and 117-118.

[10] *Letters,* I, p. 348.

[11] *Letters,* II, p. 454.

[12] *Cf.* Muriel Morris, "A Note on Wordsworth and Vaughan," *Modern Language Notes,* vol. XXXIX, pp. 187-188.

[13] See *Critique of Practical Reason,* Abbot's tr., pp. 120-121.

[14] IX, 113-122. Cited by Newton P. Stallknecht, "Wordsworth and Philosophy," *P.M.L.A.,* December 1929, p. 1142. My only criticism of this excellent article on the sources of Wordsworth's philosophy is that the author is a bit too ready to infer influence upon the basis of resemblance.

[15] See Norman Kemp Smith, *A Commentary to Kant's Critique of Pure Reason,* p. 172.

[16] *Prelude,* II, 210-232; and 1805-1806 text, XIII, 247-268.

[17] II, 220-221.

BIBLIOGRAPHY

This bibliography includes only the references actually cited in the foregoing pages.

I. PHILOSOPHICAL BACKGROUND

Babbitt (Irving), *Rousseau and Romanticism*. (Boston, Houghton Mifflin, 1919.)

Gibson (James), *Locke's Theory of Knowledge and its Historical Relations*. (Cambridge University Press, 1917.)

Hartley (David), *Observations on Man, His Frame, His Duty, and His Expectations*. Two volumes. (London, 1749, 1801, 1810). Page references are to the 1810 edition.

Jowett (Benjamin), *The Dialogues of Plato*. Five volumes. (Oxford University Press, 1924.)

Kant (Emmanuel), *Critique of Pure Reason*. Translated by F. Max Muller. (New York, Macmillan, 1922.)

Kant (Emmanuel), *Critique of Practical Reason*. Translated by Thomas Kingsmill Abbott. (London, Longmans Green, 1898.)

Locke (John), *An Essay Concerning Human Understanding*. Two volumes. (Oxford University Press, 1916.)

Milton (John), *The Poetical Works of John Milton*. Edited after the original texts by H. C. Beeching. (Oxford University Press, 1916.)

More (Henry), *The Philosophical Writings of Henry More*. Edited with introduction and notes by Flora Isabel Mackinnon. (Oxford University Press, 1925.)

Priestley (Joseph), *Miscellaneous Works*. Vol. III. (London, 1818.) Contains three essays on Hartley originally published in Priestley's abridged edition of the *Observations on Man*, 1775.

Rousseau (Jean Jacque), *Emile; or, Education*. Translated by Barbara Foxley. (Everyman's Library, Dutton, 1911.)

Spinoza (Baruch de), *Ethic*. Translated by W. Hale White; translation revised by Amelia Hutchinson Stirling. (London, Duckworth, 1899.)

Smith (Norman Kemp), *A Commentary to Kant's 'Critique of Pure Reason'*. (London, Macmillan, 1918.)

Stokoe (F. W.), *German Influence in the English Romantic Period*. (Cambridge University Press, 1926.)

Traherne (Thomas), *Centuries of Meditations.* Edited by Bertram Dobell. (London, The Editor, 1908.)

Transactions of the Wordsworth Society. "Catalogue of the Rydal Mount Library." No. 6, pp. 199-257. (Edinburgh, 1884.)

Tucker (Abraham). *The Light of Nature Pursued.* (1st ed., four volumes, London, 1765; 2nd ed., seven volumes, London, 1805.)

Whitehead (Alfred North), *Science and the Modern World.* (New York, Macmillan, 1926.)

Whittaker (Thomas), *The Neo-Platonists: A Study in the History of Hellenism.* (Cambridge University Press, 1901.)

Vaughan (Henry), *The Works in Verse and Prose Complete of Henry Vaughan, Silurist, for the First Time Collected and Edited,* by A. B. Grosart. (Blackburn, C. Tiplady and Son, 1871.)

II. THE INFLUENCE OF COLERIDGE

Complete Works. Seven volumes. Edited by W. G. T. Shedd. (New York, Harper, 1858, 1884.)

Complete Poetical Works. Two volumes. Edited by E. H. Coleridge. (Oxford University Press, 1912.)

Anima Poetae. Edited by E. H. Coleridge. (London, Heinemann, 1915.)

Aids to Reflection. Edited by Henry Nelson Coleridge. (London, W. Pickering, 1839.)

Biographia Epistolaris. Two volumes. Edited by A. Turnbull. (Bohn Library ed.: London, Bell, 1911; New York, Macmillan.)

Biographia Literaria. Two volumes. Edited by J. Shawcross. (Oxford University Press, 1907.)

The Friend: A Series of Essays, In Three Volumes. (London, Fenner, 1818.)

Letters, 1785-1834. Two volumes. Edited by E. H. Coleridge. (London, Heinemann, 1895; Boston, Houghton Mifflin.)

Table Talk. Edited by H. Morley. (Morley's Universal Library ed.: London, Routledge, 1883.)

Memorials of Coleorton. Two volumes. Edited by William Knight. (Edinburgh, 1887.) (Letters written by Coleridge and Wordsworth.)

Brandl (Alois), *S. T. Coleridge's Notizbuch aus den Jahren* 1795-1798. *Herrig's Archiv fur das studium der neureren sprachen und litteraturen.* Vols. 97-98 (1896), pp. 333-372.

Carlyon (Clement), *Early Years and Late Reflections.* Vol. I. (London, 1856.)

Cottle (J.), *Early Recollections, Chiefly Relating to the Late S. T. Coleridge.* (London, Houlston, 1837.)

De Quincey (Thomas), "Samuel Taylor Coleridge," *Works.* Edited by David Masson. Vol. II. (Edinburgh, Adam and Charles Black, 1862; reprinted, 1881.)

Gingerich (S. F.), "From Necessity to Transcendentalism in Coleridge," *Proceedings of the Modern Language Association of America,* vol. XXXV (1920), pp. 1-59.

Graham (Walter), "An Important Coleridge Letter," *Journal of English and Germanic Philology,* vol. XXI (1922), pp. 531-535.

Hazlitt (William), "My First Acquaintance With Poets," *Collected Works,* vol. XII (London, Dent, 1902-1906.)

Muirhead (John H.), *Coleridge as Philosopher.* (Macmillan, 1930.)

Rea (John D.), "Coleridge's Intimations of Immortality Through Proclus," *Modern Philology,* vol. XXVI (1928), pp. 201-213.

Snyder (Alice D.), *Coleridge on Logic and Learning, with Selections from the Unpublished Manuscripts.* (Yale University Press, 1929.)

III. WORDSWORTH

Poetical Works. Eleven volumes. Edited, with a life by W. Knight. (London, Simpkin, 1882-1889; Edinburgh, W. Paterson.)

The Poems of Wordsworth. Edited by T. Hutchinson. (Oxford University Press, 1926.) This is the text used in the foregoing pages.

The Complete Poetical Works of William Wordsworth. With an introduction by John Morley. (New York, Crowell, 1907.)

The Prelude. Edited from the manuscripts by Ernest de Selincourt. (Oxford University Press, second impression, 1928.)

Prose Works. Three volumes. Edited by A. B. Grosart. (London, Moxon, 1876.)

Prefaces and Essays on Poetry, 1800-1815, *with Notes.* Edited by George Sampson. (Cambridge University Press, 1920.)

Letters of the Wordsworth Family from 1787 *to* 1855.   Three volumes.   Edited by W. Knight.   (Boston and London, Ginn, 1907.)

Letters from the Lake Poets to Daniel Stuart. (London; printed for private circulation, 1889.)

Memorials of Coleorton. Edited by W. Knight.   (Edinburgh, 1887.)

Baldwin (Edwin Chaucey), "Wordsworth and Hermes Trismegistus," *Proceedings of the Modern Language Association of America,* vol. XXXIII (1918), pp. 235-243.

Beatty (Arthur), *William Wordsworth: His Doctrine and Art in Their Historical Relations.* (2nd ed., University of Wisconsin, Madison, 1927.)

Cerf (Barry), "Wordsworth's Gospel of Nature," *Publications of the Modern Language Association of America,* vol. XXXVII (1922), pp. 615-638.

Garrod (H. W.), *Wordsworth: Lectures and Essays.* 2nd ed., enlarged.   (Oxford University Press, 1927.)

Gingerich (S. F.), *Essays in the Romantic Poets.* (New York, Macmillan, 1924.)

Harper (G. M.), *William Wordsworth* Two volumes.   (New York, Scribner, 1923.)

Hazlitt (William), "The Spirit of the Age," "Philosophical Necessity," *Collected Works,* vol. 4.   (London, Dent, 1902-1906.)

Herzberg (Max J.), "William Wordsworth and German Literature," *Proceedings of the Modern Language Association of America,* vol. XL (1925), pp. 303-345.

Legouis (Emile), *La Jeunesse de William Wordsworth,* 1770-1798. (Paris, 1896).   English translation by J. W. Matthews, as *The Early Life of William Wordsworth.* (London, Dent, 1897, 1921.)

Merill (L. R.), "Vaughan's Influence upon Wordsworth's Poetry," *Modern Language Notes,* vol. XXXVII (1922), pp. 279-283.

Morris (Muriel), "A Note on Wordsworth and Vaughan," *Modern Language Notes,* vol. XXXIX (1924), pp. 187-188.

Pierce (Frederick E.), "Wordsworth and Thomas Taylor," *Philological Quarterly,* vol. VII (1928), pp. 60-64.

Rader (Melvin), "The Transcendentalism of William Wordsworth," *Modern Philology,* vol. XXVI (1928), pp. 169-190.

Rea (John D.), Listed under Coleridge.

Robinson (Henry Crabb), *Diary, Reminiscenses, and Correspondence.* Three volumes. Edited by T. Sadler. (London, Macmillan, 1869.)

Robinson (H. C.), *The Correspondence of Henry Crabb Robinson with the Wordsworth Circle.* Edited by Edith J. Morley. (Oxford University Press, 1927.)

Stallknecht (Newton P.), "Wordsworth and Philosophy: Suggestions Concerning the Source of the Poet's Doctrines and the Nature of His Mystical Experience," *Proceedings of the Modern Language Association of America,* vol. XLIV (1929), pp. 1116-1143.

Sneath (E. H.), *Wordsworth: Poet of Nature and Poet of Man.* (Boston and London, Ginn, 1912.)

Whitehead (A. N.), Listed under Philosophical Background.

Wordsworth (Christopher), *Memoirs of William Wordsworth.* Two volumes. (London, Moxon, 1851.)

Wordsworth (Dorothy), *Journals.* Two volumes. Edited by W. Knight. (London and New York, Macmillan, 1897.) (One volume, condensed, Macmillan, 1925.)

Wordsworthiana, A Selection of Papers Read to the Wordsworth Society. Edited by W. Knight. (London, Macmillan, 1889.)

For further information the following bibliographies on Wordsworth are to be consulted:

Bernbaum (Ernest), *Guide and Anthology of the Romantic Movement.* Vol. I. (New York, Nelson, 1930.)

The Cambridge History of English Literature. Vol. IX, pp. 448-455; vol. XII, p. 575.

Cooper (Lane), "A Survey of the Literature on Wordsworth," *Publications of the Modern Language Association of America,* vol. XXIII (1908), pp. 119-127.

Dowden (Edward), *The Poetical Works of William Wordsworth.* Vol. VII, pp. 305-358. (Aldine ed., London, Bell, 1893.)

The English Association. *Short Bibliographies of Wordsworth, Coleridge, Byron, Shelley, Keats.* English Association Pamphlet 23. (Oxford, November, 1912.)

Knight (William), In his edition of Wordsworth's *Poetical Works,* vol. VIII. (London, Paterson, 1896; New York, Macmillan.)

The Modern Humanities Research Association. *Bibliography of English Language and Literature*. Published annually, 1920 to date. (Cambridge University Press.)

The Modern Language Association of America. *American Bibliography*. Published annually, 1921 to date. In its *Publications*, March of each year.

Rice (Richard A.), *Wordsworth Since* 1916 (*with a Bibliography of Recent Books and Articles on Wordsworth*). (Northampton, Mass., Smith College, 1924.)

Poole (W. F.), "Review and Magazine Articles in Criticism of Wordsworth," *Transactions of the Wordsworth Society*, vol. I, pp. 5, 93-100. (Edinburgh, 1883?)

Woods (George Benjamin), *English Poetry and Prose of the Romantic Movement*. (Chicago, Scott, Foresman and Co., 1916.) Contains excellent bibliographies of Wordsworth, Coleridge, and of the historical and social conditions of their times.

Northup (Clark Sutherland), *A Register of Bibliographies of the English Language and Literature*. (New Haven, Yale University Press, 1925.) Lists further bibliographies on Wordsworth and Coleridge.

INDEX